Children
of the
Normal School
60 Years in El Rito, 1909–1969

Children
of the
Normal School

60 Years in El Rito, 1909–1969

Sigfredo Maestas

SUNSTONE
PRESS

SANTA FE

Sunstone books may be purchased for educational, business, or sales promotional use.
For information please write: Special Markets Department, Sunstone Press,
P.O. Box 2321, Santa Fe, New Mexico 87504-2321.

Book and Cover design ▸ Vicki Ahl
Body typeface ▸ Rockwell and Ravie
Printed on acid free paper

Library of Congress Cataloging-in-Publication Data

Maestas, Sigfredo, 1940-
  Children of the Normal School : sixty years in El Rito, 1909-1969 / by Sigfredo Maestas.
    p. cm.
  Includes bibliographical references.
  ISBN 978-0-86534-846-2 (softcover : alk. paper)
  1. Spanish American Normal School (El Rito, Rio Arriba County, N.M.)--History.
  2. Teachers--Training of--New Mexico--History. I. Title.
  LB1918.E47 2011
  370.71'178952--dc23
                        2011033818

Published in

WWW.SUNSTONEPRESS.COM
SUNSTONE PRESS / POST OFFICE BOX 2321 / SANTA FE, NM 87504-2321 /USA
(505) 988-4418 / ORDERS ONLY (800) 243-5644 / FAX (505) 988-1025

Contents

Preface

Before memory of the high school that was once at El Rito dims beyond recognition, I offer you this very brief book with some recollection of the Spanish American Normal School. This is part memoir and, more often, oral history obtained from a few dozen people. I am not a historian, but I have great appreciation for the art of the historian, and I can tell you, first, that official records of the early days of the school are sparse, and information about the students who attended the school is almost nonexistent.

I was a student at the Normal School in the mid-1950s, and I am fortunate to have lived more than a dozen years on the campus at El Rito as president of one of its successor schools, Northern New Mexico Community College. As a result of my long association with the school, I have met many, many of its people: students, teachers, and staff. A consequence of having made dozens of acquaintances and friendships, in this instance, is that these very same people have availed me of the information that I needed to construct this narrative.

Now, the notes of explanation that I owe you the reader.

In the selection of the name for this book, Children of the Normal School, I am using the definition of a child that is used by the United Nations, which is, anyone under the age of eighteen. It happened also that many of the students who came to the Normal School, both day students who walked to the campus and those of us who boarded at the school, came as small boys and girls.

I say the Normal School over and over again, because it's useful. The original campus at El Rito has been called by several names: Spanish American Normal School, until about 1948; Northern New Mexico Normal School for a brief period, until 1956; Northern New Mexico State School, on and off, until 1969; and Northern New Mexico College, for a brief period in the 1960s. After it ceased to be a high school, there came the New Mexico Technical Vocational School, to about 1977, then Northern New Mexico Community College. The campus is presently a part of Northern New Mexico College, once again. Well, you see the picture.

The use of scattered records that I collected merely provided me with names and dates, which any person examining would not find very interesting. In an isolated case, one might see a recognizable name, and be done with that. This made it incumbent for me to seek out as many individuals, Children of the Normal School and a few others, who might be able to provide recollection that, in whole, described the flavor of the times of the Normal School.

There will be some former students who will wonder why I did not contact them in the way that I did other Children of the Normal School, for purposes of this book. In a word, I wish that I could have spoken with every living former student, but, of course, it is impractical to try. My fondest hope is that I was able to capture what readers would wish for me to then successfully convey about the old school.

With regard to style, in addition to the mix of memoir and story, with its proper references, what you will notice immediately is my use of diacritical marks where needed in Spanish words and names. I hope that readers with names that require an accent, Chávez, Fernández, Gómez, Gonzáles, López, Martínez, Sánchez, and so on, like seeing their names written this way. I hope that the Nuñezes and the Peñas do, too. The newly found ability is not mine, it's technology's. There may have been special editions of the old Underwood, Royal, and IBM Selectric typewriters that would provide accents and tildes when we were growing up in New Mexico, but the ordinary ones that I saw did not. Word processing is one of the blessings of modern times, as you have heard many times.

I would suggest that readers take at least a brief look at the Appendices. The lists, although not yet complete, are the largest grouping of names and dates of students who attended the Normal School of which I am aware.

I am indebted to those individuals who would interview with me as I prepared to write. Their names are listed also.

Special thanks are due individuals with Notre Dame University and Regis College, who are listed in the interviews section, also.

In the text, I listed a few references that were of use to me as I proceeded to construct the narrative for our book. A list of those references is provided at the conclusion of the book.

1

THEY CAME FROM THE VILLAGES and small towns of northern New Mexico. Four students came from farther south in the Territory, and two students were from the Forty-Six that then comprised the United States of America. They came from Abiquiú, Alcalde, Chamita, Coyote, El Rito, Estancia, Gallina, Golden, Monero, Mountainair, Ojo Caliente, Ranchos de Taos, Roswell, Taos, Vallecitos, Velarde, and Venus. One student was from Pagosa in Colorado, and a second one called Frankfort, Kentucky her home. They came to the Spanish American Normal School at El Rito by wagon, on horseback, and on foot.

The year was 1909, and early in the first fall term there were 46 students enrolled. (Lux, G., 1984) New Mexico was still a territory of the United States, and its public educational system was yet young. Sixteen students were from El Rito, a community that had no other school. Not many of our communities in the *Río Arriba* had public schools. Those that did had one-room schoolhouses, and teachers who could barely read and write. (Wiley, T., 1965) Once they arrived in El Rito, however, students would reside and attend classes in a large new building that had been built away from the village, out on the plain of the El Rito plateau where only the gray sage-brush and a few *piñón* trees grew amidst the waving grass. The building was larger than most students had seen. We'll revisit this building again in the next few chapters.

Many of the students were interested in a general education. A few were interested in becoming teachers. None of the students were prepared to undertake any more than the elementary grades, however.

The school staff consisted of only two, both women. Mrs. George Dixon was in charge. Students had been taught at home to be respectful and to refer to their elders formally—so she was Mrs. Dixon to everyone. No one bothered to record her given name.

Students were used to the kind of life that the Normal School had to offer during its first year: no electricity, no phones, no radio, or indoor plumbing. Water was hauled in barrels from the village, since there wasn't a well on the property. Outhouses were built, his and hers, early in the first fall term. Lighting was furnished with candlelight, which students also used at home. But soon during the school year students would have lamps that burned coal oil, kerosene.

Nights could be pitch dark, except when the full moon was out, in which case their world was wonderfully lit. At times like this, boarding students would sit outside until it was time for bed, sing songs and tell stories about their homes. When they retired for the day, they could hear the coyotes howling behind their combined dormitory and classroom building, out toward the hills west of the campus.

Next day, students would forget the night before in the hustle and bustle of lining up for breakfast, and, following that, a full day of classes.

Most students had very little money. Rural people in the United States simply didn't have a lot of money. In the Territory of New Mexico there was a marked absence of cash in our villages. So students brought food that they produced on their parents' small farms: wheat and corn, beans, squash, chile, and, occasionally, meat from hogs, cattle, lambs or sheep. From the valleys of the Chama River and the Río Grande, students would bring a few pears and apples—*manzanita mejicana*, we called it—in the fall. These provisions were delivered to the school in partial payment for the students' room and board.

From the very beginning, also, boarding students did odd jobs to complete their payment for room and board. They waited on tables in the dining area, washed dishes, and, in winter, stoked the pot-bellied stoves with wood and coal. Then there was janitorial work; there was always that kind of work. Life was simple, but at El Rito life was good.

Students didn't know it then, but the school, which they were learning to appreciate and to love, would become sometimes a refuge, at other times an orphanage, but most often home for generations of youngsters, far into the future for another sixty years.

◻

I interviewed a number of former students—listed in the Appendix—in preparation for this book, but, moreover, over the years I have spoken with tens upon tens of the Children of the Normal School. I attended the Spanish American Normal School during its fifth decade, in the fifties. The Normal School about which I write lasted six decades. Those who have spoken to me about their times while in school at El Rito did so with wistfulness, invariably, and often in superlatives. I have come away from our reminiscences believing that perhaps *there are* ways in which to describe the spirit of the times, which varied from decade to decade. This is somehow worth doing; it is part of our social and cultural history.

For many boarding students "El Rito"—this is frequently how we refer to the old Normal School—was home, sometimes the only home we knew in our youth. For day students, the school year was a welcome interruption of the boredom of rural lives, familiar to many of us, most often given to farming and ranching. Many boarding students were also rural kids who were half in awe listening to our counterparts from the city talk about their urban adventures.

In my adulthood, many of the stories of El Rito remind me of tales told by Jorge Luis Borges, Gabriel García Márquez, Mark Twain, or, better yet, John Nichols, who has written about the people of northern New Mexico. Perhaps the *aura,* or the sheer magical ambience of the place, can be comprehended only by those who were there, and for us it's worth recapturing more fully. There is also a desire to disseminate the story more widely.

Narrative becomes less believable with the use of superlatives, an excessive number of adjectives and adverbs, and I try to avoid them. I'll simply tell a story as related to me by the former children of the Normal School, which leads to examination of its component parts.

The history of the Spanish American Normal School provides also an understanding of the lives and times of people of the twentieth century in northern New Mexico, in addition to telling the story of the Children of the Normal School. I'll add a brief telling of this history as well.

For the great majority of people in this region, the period between 1846, the time of the coming of the US Army of the West, and 1940s, the onset of the Second World War, were times of great plenty in terms of food to eat and a bountiful nature to explore. The same period, however, was one of great deprivation: few employment opportunities, little money, monotony of experiences, and few schools.

We knew little about boarding school. Very few people whom we knew, or knew about, had stories with which to enlighten us about boarding school. Years later, I tried to compare our modest experiences with those of boarding schools kids, both in the United States and elsewhere, for whom life was vastly different.

▣

One personality about whom we knew became our United States Senator of the early 1930s. Bronson Cutting, who resided in Santa Fé and owned the *Santa Fe New Mexican*, had been a student at Groton, the college preparatory high school in the East. Also a student at Groton had been President Franklin D. Roosevelt, who has had several biographers. An examination of their high school years amounts to reading about their struggle to succeed in the manner that rich kids out east were expected to excel. It was important that they "measure up."

They easily overcame the snobbish social environment of their school; they were, after all, boys from exceedingly wealthy families. While seldom brilliant as students, they nevertheless held their own in a competitive academic environment. Interestingly, for both of them the major struggle was to convince their peers of their athletic prowess. Sound familiar? Neither of the gentlemen had much to say about their experiences as boarding students, however. Instead, one has to go to their biographers to learn about their formative years at school.

A more informative story revolves around the person of one Eric Blair, an Englishman known more widely as George Orwell, writer. Orwell is known, among other things, for his participation during the Spanish Civil War on the side of the Republic, against Francisco Franco. Orwell the boy was a contemporary of our oldest schoolmates at the Normal School, from 1909 on up to about 1915. Now there is a guy who had a lot to say about British boarding schools, not always complimentary.

Blair's parents were Anglican, about as close to being Catholic as a Protestant gets in England. At age eight, Blair attended a school named after St. Cyprian, which he describes by another name in an essay, "Such, Such Were the Joys." These were not happy times for little Eric Blair. Those who ran the school were mean. They failed to try to understand a boy who wet the bed, and in fact they treated him as a miscreant, by beating him. George Orwell always believed that a child who wet the bed did so because he was yanked all of a sudden from a comfortable home environment to a strange place. Maybe so.

Orwell endured St. Cyprian's, but barely. He attended Wellington, briefly, then went on to Eton on scholarship. His comments about Eton are few, although he was viewed to be relatively happy there.

Eton, by the way, is one of the finest preparatory schools in the world, known formally as Eton College. It has three sister schools in England of similar ilk. Although these schools enjoy their vast reputations for excellence, they also come under suspicion for providing an unkind atmosphere for certain kids. Among unhappy products of the same schools were a couple of students who, with colleagues in university, came to be known as the Cambridge Five. The five, Anthony Blunt, Guy Burgess, John Cairnross, Donald McLean, and Kim Philby, became spies for the Soviet Union, and possibly counter spies for England as far back as the early 1940s. A couple of them, Burgess and McLean, eventually defected to the Soviet Union. What they seemed to have in common was that they attended some of these prep schools.

The popular literature and a motion picture or two have tried to deal with the disaffection of boarding students while in school, and its attendant consequences, with only mixed success. I won't speculate beyond making these observations about the differing reasons that youngsters become unhappy.

I say these things because our recollection about life at the Spanish American Normal School is considerably different. Only occasionally can I find very much in common with my known world of boarding students, but there are others of a lesser reputation with whom I may have more in common. I have mentioned only the names of widely known personalities. Occasionally, I have known a former boarding school student who shares views similar to those held by Children of the Normal School, but seldom.

The case of the Spanish American Normal School is unique, I think. This is what this book is about.

▣

Someone was responsible for this magnificent experiment that was the Spanish American Normal School. In a state in which public instruction had come into law only twenty years before, and in which the dream of universal education was still unfulfilled in and around 1910, the principle on which it was founded—that a school in El Rito should be dedicated to training teachers of Spanish-speaking children of northern New Mexico—was prescient.

Two men, in particular, should remain in our memory for having founded the Spanish American Normal School at El Rito. It turns out that one of the individuals, a former Governor of the Territory, is honored by our historians for his fine work on behalf of public and higher education in New Mexico. About this second person, little has been said, although he is the principal benefactor in establishing the Spanish American Normal School. I begin the next chapter with his story.

Venceslao Jaramillo (b. 1875–d. 1920) was a prominent rancher, merchant, legislator, and county treasurer. During a brief lifetime, he chaired the state Republican Party and was a delegate to the first Constitutional Convention of the State of New Mexico in 1912. He is one of the founders of the Spanish American Normal School at El Rito, where he resided, and provided the principal impetus toward the institution's establishment. The photograph, taken about 1897 when Jaramillo worked in the office of Territorial Governor Miguel A. Otero, shows him in a parade-ground style uniform of the Governor's militia. The picture is an original from the collection of the Rancho de Chimayó and is published here with the permission of Florence Jaramillo, proprietor.

2

A **BRIGHT YOUNG MAN**—one far ahead of his time in understanding that his people in New Mexico would need education in order to flourish in the United States of America—had been born in El Rito into the family of *don* Pedro Ignacio Jaramillo and *doña* Ana María Gallegos de Jaramillo on February 10, 1875. The Jaramillos, prominent in the community, throughout the *Río Arriba*, and in the Territory, lived up the present canyon road. A well-mannered and cultured family in which Venceslao was an only son, they had two older girls who heaped attention on their brother.

Don Pedro was a rancher and store-owner who had served in the Territorial House of Representatives in the early 1890s. *Doña* Ana María, in addition to making a comfortable home in El Rito for the Jaramillos, provided *don* Pedro a family connection to the Burns, prominent Republicans who resided in Los Ojos.

Venceslao had been tutored at home for his early schooling, and, seldom enjoying good health even as a child, he may have attended school in Santa Fe while staying with an uncle and aunt in that city in order to be close to medical care. (Jaramillo, C.M., 1955) *Don* Pedro and *doña* Ana María sought to provide Venceslao as many experiences and education as family circumstances permitted. When Venceslao was eleven years of age, his parents put him and cousin Tom Burns on the train in Lamy for the long ride to Notre Dame, the elementary school, in Indiana. Venceslao attended only one year, but it was a giant leap forward for the boy.

▣

Interviews have contributed in large measure to this narrative, as readers will learn. In this instance, it happened that, in January 2009, John Martin, an alumnus of the Normal School and son of George

J. Martin, its first president, brought me to the home in Santa Fé of his sister Roberta Martin Brosseau in search of information about Venceslao Jaramillo and his family. Roberta had been a student at the Loretto Academy during the years in which Angelina, Venceslao and Cleofas Jaramillo's daughter, was a student there. Cleofas, by now widowed, and Angelina resided in Santa Fe in that period of the early 1930s when Roberta became their close friend.

In passing, Roberta mentioned that she thought that Venceslao had attended Notre Dame. With this lead, I left Roberta's home excitedly. I called Notre Dame on the phone, and, certainly, the Notre Dame registrar's office provided records of a time in which the institution contained an elementary and high school. I owe this mention to John and Roberta for that pleasant, sunny winter afternoon that they spent with me talking about Venceslao's wife and daughter, whom she knew so well. Roberta Martin Brosseau passed away not long after we spoke.

I discovered that Venceslao Jaramillo had attended Notre Dame at the age of eleven, accompanied by his cousin Tom Burns, from Los Ojos. He was there only one year, Tom remained longer. Venceslao returned to New Mexico for a couple of years, then at age fourteen his parents again sent him away, this time to Denver, to attend a Jesuit-run boarding high school, College of the Sacred Heart. From 1889 to 1891 Venceslao attended Sacred Heart where he accelerated his studies. Venceslao Jaramillo completed the liberal arts program, excelling in English composition and History. Upon returning once again to New Mexico, Venceslao attended St. Michael's College in Santa Fe.

In 1896, at the age of 21 years, Venceslao was elected to the Territorial House of Representative in which he served two consecutive terms. At the same time, he worked on the staff of Territorial Governor Miguel A. Otero near the close of the century.

It was during the time that Venceslao Jaramillo worked in the Governor's staff that he was appointed to the New Mexico militia, available mostly on ceremonial occasions. The Governor assigned him the rank of colonel. I relate this, unimportant though it may seem to the story, because most of the existing pictures of Venceslao Jaramillo as a young man show him in the cavalry-style uniform of the militia. Florence Jaramillo, proprietor of Rancho de Chimayó and former member of the Northern New Mexico College Foundation Board, allowed me to borrow the original photograph of Venceslao Jaramillo in uniform. I made copies, one of which may be seen at Northern New Mexico College. The picture is included in this book and in *Romance of a Little Village Girl* written by Cleofas M. Jaramillo and published in 1955.

▣

Venceslao Jaramillo, 23, and Cleofas Martínez, 19, were married on July 27, 1898 after a two-year courtship. The wedding in Taos attracted much attention, both bride and groom being the son and daughter of prominent families of the *Río Arriba*. The wedding party included Tom Burns, friend, cousin, and political ally of the bridegroom, as best man. Governor Miguel Otero traveled by train from Santa Fe to Tres Piedras, and by horse drawn wagon to Taos from there, in order to attend the wedding.

▣

The train by which people traveled from Santa Fé to points north, including Española, Embudo, Tres Piedras, and Antonito, Colorado was known popularly as the Chili Line. This facilitated travel a lot, especially for anyone with money, which would have excluded most of our students attending at El Rito. Students of early railroad travel through our small towns and villages may wish to read Governor Otero's memoir for an interesting story of his trip by rail to the Jaramillos' wedding.

Sometime during the Jaramillos' courtship, Venceslao purchased a phaeton, which was a fancy buggy at the time, pulled by a team of horses. This was their mode of travel near their wedding day. After they were married, on occasion, one or the other of the couple would be delivered to Barranca, which is north of Embudo and up on the *mesa* above the Río Grande. From here, Santa Fé could be made by train after a very long day from El Rito, using two conveyances. They would leave El Rito about six in the morning, and arrive at Barranca close to noon. The remaining part of the journey required about five hours to Santa Fé, if the train was on time. Eleven to twelve hours from El Rito to Santa Fé seems an ordeal today, but it was more desirable than the longer trip via Española.

Train travel was not common. The route covered Santa Fé to Española, then past Embudo a few miles before it rose to the still underpopulated plateau that includes Barranca, Taos Junction, and Tres Piedras, before arriving in Antonitio, Colorado. Travel was slow, less than twenty miles an hour, closer to fifteen. And few local people had money, a second complication.

The train also carried produce from the valleys around Española, lots of *chile*—hence the name Chili Line—and logs from La Madera. The D&RG, as it was known, added a spur to La Madera, for this latter purpose. It found itself with insufficient business, however, as railroads all across the US started feeling competition from the trucking industry. The Denver and Río Grande Railroad Company eventually went broke with the Chili Line, and the company removed the rails, beginning in 1941.

◻

It was while in the House of Representatives that Venceslao, always precocious as a child, made powerful friends in the Capitol, in the legislature, in Santa Fé, and throughout the Territory. He became known for his even temper, his intellect, and, most importantly, his ability to hear all sides on important questions and to achieve concurrence on their resolution. He managed to earn the respect and friendship of Governor Miguel A. Otero and L. Bradford Prince, a former Territorial Governor, who was an avowed opponent of Otero. Although Otero and Prince were of the same party, Republican, they quarreled bitterly during the time that Otero was governor. But Venceslao tended to make things well for Republicans, thereby helping the party to hold on to its political advantage in this state. His popularity increased for the skill that he demonstrated in keeping peace within his party, and in 1911 he was made chairman of the

Republican Party of New Mexico, no small accomplishment for a thirty-six year old from the remote village of El Rito.

The important friendship for Venceslao, in our story, is with L. Bradford Prince. Venceslao Jaramillo had nurtured the dream of a school at El Rito for a long time, and while in the House of Representatives, he tried to promote a bill to found a campus in El Rito. He was unsuccessful. Governor Otero was not interested in education for the masses in the manner that Govenor Prince had demonstrated earlier in the 1890s. Governor Prince had been largely responsible for establishing the superintendent's office for public schools in 1891, and he had supported establishing universities in 1889. When Venceslao Jaramillo sought to establish a normal school in El Rito, during his second term in the House and Otero's term as governor, all that the legislature and the governor would permit him to have were funds to build a building to locate the New Mexico Reformatory School there. With foresight, he accepted the money that was appropriated—and then he waited.

By the fall of 1908, Venceslao was well established in his businesses as rancher and storeowner, as his father had been before him. In the legislature, as Senator from the *Río Arriba*, was L. Bradford Prince, who resided in Chamita. Venceslao Jaramillo saw an opportunity developing in the legislature and the Office of the Territorial Governor; he might possibly be able to get a bill approved for the establishment of the Spanish American Normal School at El Rito, if former Governor Prince agreed to introduce and promote the bill in the Assembly. Venceslao could count on additional influential friends, all Republicans, to assist with this effort: Charles Spiess, Chairman of the Council (Senate) from Las Vegas; Hermengildo Vigil, representing Río Arriba, resided in Velarde: Epimenio A. Miera from Cuba in Sandoval County; a new Republican Governor in the person of George Curry; and T.D. Burns and John Sargent, both prominent in Republican party politics. He could also count on the previously constructed building in El Rito, still unoccupied.

The key to Venceslao Jaramillo's success was his, and L. Bradford Prince's, knowledge, experience, and political acumen. They knew that the business establishment and prominent politicians desired statehood. State government was aware of the zeal with which joining the Union was awaited, and it was willing to do everything possible to ensure statehood. The nation saw New Mexico as a territory inhabited largely by Indians and Mexicans, foreign-speaking, by their reckoning, and this popular impression, often fueled by the pulp-fiction market, had to be tempered.

Senator L. Bradford Prince introduced a bill in the 1909 legislative Council that stated that a school, to be known as the Spanish American Normal School, was to be founded at El Rito to train teachers who would dedicate their efforts to teaching Spanish-speaking students in the Territory. On the last day of the legislative session during that year, the bill was approved and signed by Governor George Curry, a Republican also.

Thus the Spanish American Normal School was founded. The facts concerning the times and events that preceded its establishment are indisputable. They have been told in several ways by differing authors, but seldom in acknowledging the credit that is due Venceslao Jaramillo.

◻

I was a boy at the school in 1954—it had been renamed the Northern New Mexico Normal School, a name that we all liked—when the new high school building was dedicated to the memory of Venceslao Jaramillo. Clory B. Tafoya was superintendent; Facundo Rodríguez was principal; and, Edwin L. Mechem was Governor of the State. They participated in the ceremony, one that everyone present enjoyed. Jaramillo Hall, newly named, has served the campus well since that time.

One has to wonder why it took almost a half century for the school to recognize the debt of gratitude that it owed to Venceslao Jaramillo for its founding. Also, why it is that the work of Governor L. Bradford Prince has yet to be acknowledged formally by the school.

Two reasons stand out: first, neither the school nor the state of New Mexico has amply recited the history of the Normal School. This narrative about its Children will address only briefly what the institution has been, and should be, in relation to the intention of its two principal founders. In another manuscript I explore more fully the purpose, successes, and failures of this school now past a century in age.

A second reason points to the strength and weakness, sadly, of politics in these United States. The deeds of Venceslao Jaramillo were recognized, good and well, in 1954. Not very much was said, or has been mentioned since, about Governor Prince. You would ask, why is this? In a few words, politics in northern New Mexico has been dominated since 1932 by Democrats. Venceslao Jaramillo and L. Bertrand Prince were Republicans. It was no coincidence that in 1954 when this well-deserved recognition was granted to Jaramillo, Governor Mechem and the NNMNS administration were also Republican.

Would the opposite have ensued, i.e., would recognition have come earlier if the allegiances of Jaramillo and Prince to party had been different? Probably.

Would the opposite party have been so callous in ignoring the merits of persons not of their persuasion? Probably.

This is politics in these United States, and especially in New Mexico. *¿Que haremos?*

▣

I assert that Venceslao Jaramillo is the principal founder of the Spanish American Normal School, which no other authors have done to my knowledge. It's easy to ignore some facts that point to the founding of the school at El Rito as the singular greatest accomplishment of one man, although many of the same facts are indisputable.

First, his wife mentions in her memoirs, at least twice, the burning desire of her husband to establish a school in El Rito to help the poor people of northern New Mexico, the *Río Arriba*, to advance. After it was established, she quotes him expressing that his fond dream had come true: the Spanish American Normal School.

Venceslao Jaramillo visited with former Governor L. Bradford Prince in Santa Fé in November 1908, prior to the legislative session in which the now Senator Prince would introduce the bill to establish the

Normal School. No doubt Jaramillo may have discussed Republican Party politics or other concerns in the public realm with Prince. But could anything have been of greater importance to Venceslao Jaramillo than his campus at El Rito?

I point out earlier in this chapter the support that Venceslao Jaramillo enjoyed among legislators, and especially members of his own party. Needless to say, Venceslao had "his ducks in line."

For a brief while, Jaramillo served as regent of a New Mexico reformatory school, and presided over a building in El Rito intended for an intitution that never came to be. The building, authorized in 1903, was still vacant in 1908. The following year, the building was occupied by the Spanish American Normal School. Historians like to skirt the issue of Venceslao's design in this matter, and by inference, the complicity of Governor Prince and members of their party.

The first twenty acres on which the Spanish American Normal School resided were donated by Venceslao and Cleofas M. Jaramillo and William Sargent, of El Rito, in a signed deed in 1903.

In 1909 in the absence of an executive officer, L. Bradford Prince and Venceslao Jaramillo held matters affecting the school together by serving on its first Board of Regents, together with Melaquías Martínez, Squire Hart, and John Sloan. Prince and Jaramillo resided in Río Arriba County; others in the counties of Taos and Santa Fé. Prince and Jaramillo ran the school during this first year, hiring teachers and maintenance staff needed to open the school's doors.

Jaramillo's health, seldom very strong, suffered in those years immediately after 1912. He had to travel El Rito to Tierra Amarilla to Santa Fe often, to Board meetings and to his job as County Treasurer. The dedication of the man was unmatched in the annals of the Normal School.

◨

Venceslao and Cleofas Jaramillo traveled widely within the United States, to parts reachable by train. They acquired properties in Chama and in Denver, Colorado. They also built a beautiful house in El Rito, which many of us saw and read about in the *Denver Post.*

Venceslao and Cleofas had three children, but only a daughter, Angelina, survived beyond childhood. Angelina's tragic death in Santa Fé in fall 1931 is a story that I shall not retell. Instead readers are referred to *Justice Betrayed*, written by Ralph Melnick and published in 2002.

Venceslao, much admired by his wife, is the subject of the first part of her memoir, *Romance of a Little Village Girl*. While he lived, he pleased her greatly and served to fortify her *nuevo mejicano* values. He died at a very early age, 45, in a Denver hospital on May 20, 1920, as the man who would—unknowingly perhaps—influence the lives of several hundred Children of the Normal School.

3

HARD TIMES BESET THE NORMAL SCHOOL throughout its first decade. It should have been a forewarning of things to come for those in charge. Few people understood that difficulties facing the school would persist for a long time. Not that seeing the clear signs of adversity helped the school, since more often it tended to discourage the school's administration.

Children of the Normal School, on the other hand, were pleased with their school and only on rare occasion would they find reason to be unhappy, or worse yet, to despair. Those who ran the school during this tough period, 1909–1919, managed to keep from students their own anxieties about the poor state in which the school found itself. I'll comment but briefly, later in this book, about successes and failures of administration(s) of the school, with one or two exceptions, because, after all, this is not the history of the school (that I am writing elsewhere), but the story of its students. They deserve their own story, with only incidental mention of the operation of the school.

◻

The first president—superintendent was sometimes the title given the chief executive—was George J. Martin, a graduate of Manhattan College, whose campus was still situated on the island that gives New York City its magnificence. A young man in his early twenties, George Martin would hold his first job in El Rito. He came to the Normal School in 1910 for the start of the school's second year.

Of the first three years of the Normal School, no records are left concerning students. Since no official records remain at the school concerning any of those who attended elementary or high school, information concerning the earliest years of the school is almost nonexistent. George Martin was quite clear, however, about the circumstances facing the first children of the Normal School and the worth of their accomplishments. In correspondence with regents, the governor, and anyone who would listen, he pointed out that students were not prepared to tackle advanced schoolwork, as anyone who knows about New Mexico in the early twentieth century would guess. On top of that, he said, attendance in early fall and late spring was irregular because students had to be back on the farm helping with the work. In spite of this, the Normal School did train almost fifty teachers during his first few years as president. Martin also praised students for their effort and accomplishments, and for overcoming the less-than-desirable academic environment that circumstances created.

Martin met with luck, good and bad, soon after his arrival in New Mexico. Martin was a well-educated man, said to be fluent in English, Spanish, French, and German. His major back at Manhattan was in Modern Languages, according to that school. Although he possessed an ability to manage, he had to be disheartened to learn that he would spend the large part of his day teaching students at an elementary level. The staff was very small; George Martin had no choice but to teach a full load of classes.

Good luck emerged in another form to bolster his spirits. George Martin married Margaret Allen at St. Francis Cathedral in Santa Fé on September 30, 1912. Ms. Allen was a nurse at St. Vincent Hospital where George had been a patient earlier.

The couple made a good team especially evident in November of 1912 when the school building burnt. That was the worst luck imaginable for the school. Readers may try to imagine the difficulty of placing forty to fifty boarders in homes around El Rito. Some of them lived with George and Margaret; matters concerning their health were in the care of Ms. Martin, the nurse.

George J. Martin was president four years. I have found nothing to indicate that the Board of Regents, or anyone associated with the Spanish American Normal School, had reason to be dissatisfied with Martin's job performance. He simply grew tired of the job that the presidency of the Normal School had turned out to be, and the inability or unwillingness of the state to provide better support for the institution. George Martin resigned from the job and left the Normal School in order to move to Pueblo, Colorado.

The Martins returned to El Rito in 1923, according to their son, John, and went into business with John Sargent, buying and selling sheep and wool. Eventually they opened up the Martin Store, a landmark in El Rito for a long time, which sold groceries and dry goods.

The Martin family included in time a daughter, Roberta, and four sons, Tom, George, John, and Pat. Roberta studied at Loretto Academy in Santa Fé; the boys became Children of the Normal School.

George Martin had provided the Normal School a measure of stability, greatly necessary for schools but often not forthcoming. The school was moderately successful in producing graduates who would and could teach. After its first year, the Spanish American Normal School placed ten teachers in this region—in those days teachers often possessed education not much beyond grade six—but demand for teachers far outstripped the number that the school could produce. Interestingly, if we examine that job market today, a shortage of teachers in New Mexico persists.

After Martin left, the Normal School entered its darkest period in trying to maintain a qualified staff, and in maintaining stability necessary for progress of the school. Between 1914 and 1919 the school had no fewer than five presidents. One of these presidents, out of frustration, acquiesced to his Board of Regents in recommending to the Governor of the State that the school be closed. Fortunately for Children of the Normal School, Governor Washington Lindsey demurred. This unprecedented occurrence was in winter 1919. Dr. Guillermo Lux, in his book written in 1984 for Northern New Mexico Community College, tells this story well.

If it is always darkest before the dawn, then for the Normal School one of its new days occurred, immediately following the past fiasco, with the arrival of Filadelfio Baca in fall 1919. The gentleman, from Santa Fé, knew public education. He had been assistant superintendent for public instruction, and possessed knowledge of vocational agriculture.

Expansion of educational programs to include a high school at the Normal School had been discussed, and some planning had been done during the previous administration. A high school still did not exist in fall 1919, however. Baca ordered that class offerings beyond eighth grade be expanded, and in spite of a low number of students, the school proceeded to offer the courses deemed necessary without delay.

For several years, I had been interested in Filadelfio Baca. Who was he? What possessed him of the ability to create the high school? What happened to him? People in El Rito and its environs were always helpful to me in trying to understand our history, but no one remembered Filadelfio Baca.

In 1998, during a large reunion of our alumni at El Rito—I was president of Northern New Mexico Community College then—I met Joe and Sue Baca, who were residing in Manhattan Beach, California at the time, and came for the reunion. Joe Baca is one of the Children of the Normal School. Filadelfio Baca was Joe and Sue's uncle. They had information that, coupled with other leads, permitted me to gain great appreciation for the work of this man.

In another manuscript that I have hinted about, I have a more complete story of Filadelfio Baca; it is recognition that he deserves. This story, however, is about how Children of the Normal School were affected by good deeds of their school, administrators, and teachers. The next decade in it begins with the presidency of Filadelfio Baca and the high school.

4

THE NEW HIGH SCHOOL IN THE 1920S would help to
accelerate growth of the campus. Did I say campus? There was only
one large building, rebuilt after the fire of 1904, and a couple of smaller
structures, for living and dining. The campus was still pretty desolate.
Leopoldo J. Romero, in *'El Cambio' Mural*, done in charcoal, depicts
the pastoral ambience surrounding school buildings about this time.
Sheep could still come up to the door of the school. This would change
at the end of the 1920s. More new small buildings and a gymnasium,
the pride of people of those times, were constructed on the north end
of the property.

The school population would change, also. The Children of
the Normal School would become an increasingly better educated
group, a bit more sophisticated in the ways of the world, in spite of the
continued isolation of the campus.

▣

Isolation of people in the region of the Spanish American
Normal School, and points north, provided for unsurpassed tranquility
and absence of danger. Down in the valley of the Río Grande, since the
1880s, the Chili Line had brought an amount of commerce to the area.
The fact that the train carried some passengers, meant that tourists,
or strangers to the area touring by, left and took away some cultural
impressions. But this was limited to villages along the railway.

World War I had come and gone without causing too much alarm,
although as a state New Mexico contributed a disproportionately high
number of participants in that war. Other occurrences, in Europe and
in the United States, were of little consequence. The Versailles treaty,
by which England, France, Italy, and the United States tried to curb
German aggression, had some adverse consequences that people

here knew little about. What did it matter that money that Germans had in the early twenties became worthless? Did it matter that a demagogic man of despicable character named Adolph Hitler was beginning to be known in provincial Germany, Bavaria , as a result of increasing poverty in that country, perhaps? Probably not. Even today, when news flash across the world in seconds, it's difficult to discern and anticipate danger. In 1920s New Mexico, the pace of life was slow, its manner of living was placid.

Life in urban United States, as described by Frederick Lewis Allen in *Only Yesterday*, his book about the 1920s published in 1931, was based on affluence largely unknown in this region. Besides, the effect of new innovations was always slow in getting here. Witness the emergence of the automobile, first introduced in 1908 by Henry Ford as the Model T. It would be a while before *any* cars were seen in El Rito.

◳

The road from Abiquiú up to El Rito was a rough dirt track. Some of the older members of the community can remember a couple of cars in the village. One of them was a Buick, owned by George Martin, which John A. Martin recalls. Sometime after 1925, the school purchased a truck to haul provisions from the Valley; it served, also, to shuttle boys and girls basketball teams to play ball in nearby communities. This period, seen as the Roaring Twenties in more affluent parts of America, signaled modernization that would barely touch El Rito and the Normal School.

In public education, vast change would begin. In 1923, comprehensive legislation was passed in Santa Fé creating the new School Code. According to Tom Wiley's *Public School Education in New Mexico*, published in 1965, this act enabled the start of new high schools, authorized by county commissions around the state. New regulations mandated the certification of teachers by examination, or, important for the Spanish American Normal School, by earning credential in the form of institutional credits. This gave rise to means by which the state department of education, in consultation with normal schools and universities, would begin to certify teachers.

With the creation of the new high school, the Normal School at El Rito began to ease into the state's new method for certifying teachers. In addition to the general education program, the school offered introductory courses in pedagogy, history and foundations of education, educational psychology, and teaching methods, very similar to courses offered to teachers today.

Sadly for all of us, even for those who did not know Filadelfio Baca, he died on January 26, 1923 at age 57 after a sudden and brief illness. He had accelerated the progress of the Normal School during his brief years as president, and the school would no longer elicit questions about its usefulness and worth to the state, until many years later. In the meantime, the Spanish American Normal School became known primarily as a thriving high school, tucked away in the foothills of northern New Mexico.

An innovation that Baca brought to the Normal School was vocational education, as one would guess from his background. This, too, would play an important role in the future of the school.

◻

Laura Redman was the high school's first graduate, in 1922. I met her at my installation as president in summer 1985, when she gave me her diploma to be placed in the office of the president at El Rito.

It was but a brief visit with Laura Redman Dougherty, and so I had to learn about her from two of her children, Larry Parcell in Arizona and Hydia María Dougherty of Santa Fé. Laura Redman had been born in Pagosa Springs, Colorado, on April 20, 1903 and moved to El Rito with her family while still a girl of ten years. Meade Martin, John's son, allowed me to listen to an old tape recording in which Laura's twin brother Lawrence spoke. Lawrence had also attended the Normal School. The intricate social web up here in these hills has been most helpful in bringing to light information about people of the early twentieth century, their lives and times.

Laura Redman attended Highlands University and the University of New Mexico after graduation at the Normal School. In 1929, she was back in El Rito teaching first grade. A photograph of

Laura and her first grade class are included in this book.

Laura Redman Dougherty earned plaudits for her work at the García Street School in Santa Fé in her later life. Recognition was afforded her for being able to simultaneously teach parents and her kindergarteners.

◙

After the passing of Filadelfio Baca, José Jordi became president, in 1923. Some of our friends in El Rito remember Jordi, a Spaniard, probably from Catalunya. Although Jordi is only slightly better remembered than Baca, both presidents of the decade of the twenties earned high praise for the job that they did at the Normal School. Jordi was at the Normal four years.

John V. Conway, prominent businessman and converted educator, followed as president and finished out the remainder of the decade of the 1920s. The high school had grown to about 45 students after a new dormitory was erected during Filadelfio Baca's last year.

Conway, which is how he was known, was a strong educator who started offering a few courses at a time toward the creation of a junior college. He was a former superintendent of public instruction, and very knowledgeable about requirements for preparation of teachers.

◙

The high school gained impetus and in 1923 three students graduated, followed by seven more graduates in 1924. The high school was here to stay, if there had been any doubt.

One of the graduates in 1923 was Sixto Valdez, who taught in the Rio Arriba County Schools and went on to become assistant county school superintendent.

I knew Sixto Valdez when I was a boy. I remember him as a fairly tall, slender man with gray hair and mustache, but I had to learn about him from his daughter Helen and son Eli, also graduates of the Normal School. Their mother was the former Mercedes Martínez of La Madera, also a graduate of the Spanish American Normal School. Sixto and Mercedes had met while they were both attending New Mexico Highlands University, in furtherance of their teaching credentials.

Sixto was born in Los Brazos in April 1900. In his adulthood, Sixto was no stranger in rural villages, having resided in places like Cumbres, north of Chama, where his father, *don* Clemente Valdez , worked for the Denver & Río Grande Railroad Company. Sixto Valdez taught in the rural schools of Río Arriba County for about 19 years, before undertaking other jobs: principal at Ojo Caliente and, of course, that of superintendent. He also worked in the office of Public School Finance in Santa Fé, and finished his career while teaching in Tierra Amarilla.

Mercedes Martínez Valdez passed away in 1965.

Sixto moved to Albuquerque and joined *La Compañía de Treato de Albuquerque*, starring in the play *"Si Hay Posada."* He died three years ago.

◙

No amount of attention devoted to the lives of individuals like Laura and Sixto, standard bearers among Children of the Normal School who became teachers in a time when they were so badly needed, is too much. But there are many more like them, and many whom I did not know, or knew very little about. Some of these names are included in an Appendix, which I invite the reader to see.

◙

Lawrence Redman graduated with the class of 1924, he together with Anita Arellano, Pablo Forés, Bolivar Martínez, José B. Trujillo, Lafayette Varela, and Cornelio Vigil. Laura and Lawrence's brother, Glenn, also graduated at the Normal School in the year 1923, between the twins. I asked why the younger sister graduated before an older brother. The reply was that the boys had to work and earn money while Laura was preparing to be a teacher.

Lawrence attended New Mexico Highlands University where he met Cecilia C. de Baca. They married; Cecilia became the teacher in the family. She joined the faculty of the Spanish American Normal

School in late 1920s, during John Conway's administration. She taught at El Rito for five years during which Lawrence was employed in Española.

The Redman couple had several children. Michael Redman, a dentist in Española married the former Mary Ellen Montoya, who taught at the Northern New Mexico Normal School in 1949–1951.

Generations of the Redmans have resided in Española since the early twentieth century. Beginning with Laura and Lawrence, the family has been linked with the Normal School at various times.

◻

The graduating class of 1929 included seven people, only one of whom I knew. They distinguished themselves as school teachers for at least a part of their lives. Their names and place of origin are Simmie Atencio, Santa Cruz; Pauline Goddard, El Rito; Richard Ortega, Chimayó; Olive Parker, El Rito: Raymundo Romero, Vadito; Cruz Trujillo, Chimayó; and José M. Valdez, McPhee, Colorado.

I knew José Valdez also when I was a boy. Mr. Valdez was a quiet, thoughtful person who lived in the community of Lyden with his family. The Normal School listed in its records that he was from Colorado. In fact, many *nuevo mejicanos* left home to seek temporary employment, which I believe José Valdez did.

His children were my schoolmates at the public school in Velarde. Joe, Barbara, and Connie later became Children of the Normal School, also.

◻

Raymundo Romero was class valedictorian. A teacher, he lived and taught in Vadito almost his entire adult life. He and his wife Orcibiana (Anne) were married 67 years and had five children. Raymundo is featured as one of the state's notable elders, I am told, in a year 2000 issue of the New Mexico Magazine. Most of what I know about Mr. Romero was told to me by Joe Valdez, class of 1954, his nephew.

◨

Pauline Goddard, whom I did not know, was the older sister of Jane Goddard García who lives a short way down the road from the campus at El Rito. Pauline and Jane were both Children of the Normal School. Their father was John Goddard from Kansas; their mother was Augusta Carrillo Goddard from Roswell. Pauline followed in the steps of an older sister, Genevieve, also a graduate of the Normal School and a teacher in the rural schools. Pauline taught elementary school in Gallina and Ensenada and other villages in northern New Mexico.

◨

Olive Parker, member of the class of 1929, I would have had no way of knowing, or knowing about, had it not been for another one of those lucky episodes that occurred while I was writing this book.

Olive Parker was born in Mancos, Colorado in 1910 and grew up in Albuquerque after her family moved there.

In the late 1920s, Olive enrolled at the Normal School to prepare for a career in teaching. Olive had a younger sister who also enrolled at the school. Olive and Marguerite were very good students. Olive was an unusually photogenic young woman; witness her picture with the class of 1929.

One winter day a woman called on the telephone and told me she is Katie Bateman Allison, and she had read in the *Río Grande Sun* that I was working on a book about the Normal School. Did I know who she was? And could she and her husband Dana visit with me? Of course, I remembered her from some of the school yearbooks of the Normal School and the name Bateman was well known in El Rito. She and Dana visited with me a couple of times.

Katie showed me some photographs, and other memorabilia involving Dana. They were both Children of the Normal School.

She then proceeded to tell me about her mother, a woman named Olive Parker, whom she had not known because Olive had died at the age of 25 following childbirth, a day after Katie's slightly younger brother was born. But she had a photograph, which Katie treasured that included John Conway, the school president; Marguerite; Olive; Ernest

Baca; Ronzo Bateman; and Albert Bateman, Olive's future husband and Katie's father. Katie told me that she thought Olive had graduated at the Normal School in 1929.

I said to Katie, "Wait here." I went into my office and got out the picture of the class of 1929. "Here is your mom," I said to Katie.

I delight in telling this story, poignant though it is. The photo of the class of 1929 is one of the better ones of the first twenty years of the Spanish American Normal School. I came via this picture twice: Jane García had it because her sister Pauline Goddard is in it, and Joe Valdez allowed me to copy an original because his father was in the class.

In later chapters, I discuss Dana and Katie Allison.

◻

Rural societies tend to be quite insular the world over. There is no reason not to be. Everything that we need is immediately around us. Unless worldly for other reasons, we not only do not need our far neighbors, we can sometimes be disdainful of them. *¿Qué haremos?* This describes much of the human specie.

In the case of early twentieth century *nuevo mejicanos*, there was a second reason. Spanish had been the dominant language in our communities, only slightly affected by the coming of the Army of the West (1846). Seventy years later, give or take a few, not a whole lot had changed in this respect. In our homes parents stressed the need to learn English, in order to get along, get a job, and get a paycheck. There the matter ended. Although our parents were supremely patriotic, the matter of how the USA and its government functioned was not of great concern. In this case, the condition was not out of disrespect; on the contrary, it owed to people's supreme faith in the democracy in which they now lived.

This situation existed on up to the end of World War II, about 1945, to mark a date. Many of us are old enough to have a clear recollection of this time.

Entertainment and cultural affairs in rural communities centered around feast days, weddings, baptisms, and the like. Music, what was said at the church, public and private discourse, all were in

Spanish. I speak primarily about those of us who were poor, but the more well-to-do behaved similarly.

Popular radio didn't make its presence until much later, primarily because there was no electricity with which to operate receivers. Movies were too new to have a significant influence. A lot of people didn't read, or didn't care to read subtitles that came with the first "silents." Besides, in the villages there were no electricity, no phones, no radios, not many cars, few roads, and a consumer market that was miniscule. Entertainment was home grown: baseball and basketball games, occasional horse racing, card games, gambling, music, dancing, long walks, and picnics. Reading material, outside of the occasional newspaper, was scarce.

At the Spanish American Normal School, teachers sought to emphasize the use of English, but Spanish was the language of the playground. Children like my friends John Martin and Jane Goddard García became fluent in Spanish, as a result.

▣

Under the leadership of Filadelfio Baca, José Jordi, and John Conway the Spanish American Normal School thrived as the decade ended. The Children of the Normal School were pleased with a lot about their school; the completion of a new gymnasium was one reason.

This trio of presidents represented similar backgrounds and aspirations for the school. They introduced, as part of the vocational program of the school, an emphasis in folk arts of northern New Mexico for which the school became known. Wood products and woven rugs and tapestries were produced at the Normal School in quantities that gave the school the appearance of a small factory.

Criticism was leveled at the administration of John Convway for the exploitation of students in producing these beautiful items. Nonsense. This was a case of pure politics. Members of opposite political parties would find occasion to point, usually falsely, at wrongs that the other was perpetrating at the school. This is one of the better examples of the needling by one political party of another that went on.

The making of fine products, Spanish colonial furniture, Río Grande style rugs, tapestries, *bultos, retablos*, and similar products has been one of the hallmarks of the institution up to and including modern times.

George J. Martin became the first president of the Spanish American Normal School in mid-summer 1910, the school's second year of operation. Martin came to El Rito and the Normal School from Manhattan College in New York where he had obtained a degree in Modern Languages. This picture was taken about twenty-five years after Martin's presidency. Photograph is courtesy of Mike Martin.

Laura Redman, the first graduate of the high school, is shown here in 1929 with her first grade class in El Rito. In the picture are Top row: Mack Scarborough, unidentified, Ventura Romero, George Martin, Aniceto Varoz, Matías Ávila, John A. Martin, unidentified. Middle row: unidentified, unidentified, unidentified, unidentified, Dan Goddard, unidentified, Moises Herrera, unidentified, Lucy Silva. Bottom row: unidentified, Jane Goddard, Rosina Chávez, Mary Agnes Martínez, Isabel Jaramillo, Alice Varoz, Laura Redman Dougherty. Photograph is courtesy of John A. Martin.

The graduating class of 1929 included Raymond Romero, Vadito; Pauline Goddard, El Rito; Richard Ortega, Chimayó; Olive Parker, El Rito; José M. Valdez, McPhee, Colorado; Simmie Atencio, Santa Cruz; and Cruz Trujillo, Chimayó. Sitting is Isabel Ward, class sponsor. Photograph is courtesy of Jane Goddard García and Joe Valdez.

5

OUT OF THE PERIOD OF THE GREAT DEPRESSION
emerged a campus to build a dream on, to borrow from a great song
written in 1935 by Bert Kalmar, Harry Ruby, and Oscar Hammerstein
II. Like the song, the Spanish American Normal School grew and
grew in appeal. The song made a big splash in 1951 when sung by
Louis Armstrong; the campus's beauty, it's very quality, ambience and
aura, peaked in 1951 and then slid...and slid. Nineteen fifty-one is
considerably later in this story, however; the thirties were the time in
which the campus began to flower.

▣

The Normal School finished the 1920s in winning fashion. John
V. Conway began to make changes in line with the legislated mission
of the Spanish American Normal School. In addition to the high school,
there were courses similar to those offered in comprehensive junior
colleges in other states. In the USA, junior colleges got their start in
the 1880s and 1890s, and many were well established by 1930. We
can be certain that John Conway was well familiar with them, and
that he felt they offered what was needed in northern New Mexico:
general education, vocational courses, and introductory courses in
professional education for those seeking to become teachers.

The Normal School offered courses in line with other junior
colleges. Especially important was the fact that the new offerings
made it resemble a normal school, that is, a teachers' college.

The school administration and its Board of Regents were very
considerate of its students, charging no tuition and continuing to allow
the majority of students to work in order for them to contribute toward
their board and room. The school catalog was brief, nicely written,
and tended to exaggerate the beauty of the region and, especially, its

accessibility. In fact, the road up from the turnoff to Abiquiú was rough, a real washboard.

◙

A series of events occurred that would alter the path that the Spanish American Normal School would take after the early part of this decade. First, the political complexion of northern New Mexico changed with the election of Franklin D. Roosevelt in 1932 as President of the United States. Northern New Mexico followed suit and became a Democratic stronghold. In New Mexico, ever since statehood was achieved in 1912, people had allowed about equal numbers of Republican and Democratic Governors, and in 1931 Governor Arthur Seligman, a Democrat, took office. This meant that the Board would have three Democrats and two Republicans, likely, during his term. He appointed a native of Abiquiú, Joseph B. Grant, to the Board of which he became chairman.

President Conway was Republican, and he was fired. But there is more than the matter of political party to the conflict that developed between Conway and the Board of Regents. The Board wanted the high school to emphasize vocational instruction, and for the Normal School to deemphasize the junior college and its offerings in pedagogy. There is clear evidence of this in correspondence between one member of the Board, Regent Margaret Lane, from Albuquerque, and the Office of the Governor. The end result was that the Board removed John V. Conway from the presidency, and appointed Joseph B. Grant. The die was cast. The Spanish American Normal School became a high school emphasizing vocational education: in time, it offered, auto mechanics, beauty culture, business and secretarial courses, carpentry and woodworking, weaving, home economics and a smattering of other vocational courses. The experiment involving the junior college ended with Conway's departure, for the time being.

◙

Joe Grant is how he was known statewide. In El Rito no one

called him by his first name, and he was mostly Gráhn-teh, with a rolling 'r' to complete our Spanish rendition of the name.

Grant was not an educator; his background was in bookkeeping and accounting. He became an expert politician who exerted the most remarkable influence in creating a real campus, with a definite footprint, buildings that followed an architectural theme, well-designed walkways and vehicular paths, and a defined border of the campus. When I saw the campus for the first time in 1953, the most striking feature was the series of rock walls, to resemble something maybe out of Ireland. Many trees, silver maple and elm, lilac bushes, hardy grass, and play areas for basketball and tennis graced the campus. There were also some rock monuments that at one time must have been gorgeous with their water fountains. Rose gardens surrounded one of the monuments on the south side and in front of the president's home.

Joe Grant became friends with E.D. Trujillo and Carlos Manzanares, two of our more able politicians in Río Arriba County, and the three men shaped the political landscape in this state's northernmost Democratic stronghold.

Joe Grant's political acumen enabled him to attract federal money to construct the campus during the depression years of the mid-1930s. Overnight the Spanish American Normal School went from its pastoral ambience to one of a cozy little campus, recognizable to people coming up the road as it emerged on the foothills of the El Rito basin.

Most of the major buildings were constructed prior to 1950, in an architectural style of a Pueblo and Moorish hybrid, with earth tones in their exteriors. Jaramillo Hall is a major building constructed later, in 1953; Grant Gymnasium was completed in 1957.

Two other characteristics were attractive: the rock walls and foundations of some buildings done in similar rock and concrete. The second were paintings done by WPA-era artists, so-called, composed by artists who were supported by the Workers Project Administration during those economically difficult days of the Great Depression.

The work on campus benefited people by bringing much

needed jobs to El Rito at a time in which there was still very little money.

◻

Work on the campus progressed very slowly. To the Children of the Normal School, changes were barely perceptible, except possibly in four-year increments. If a student came in ninth grade, yes, perhaps, by the time he or she graduated, change became satisfyingly obvious.

Cutting Hall is a case in point. This edifice, built to house a women's residence, dining hall, and a small auditorium—done in familiar northern New Mexico style, with plastered walls, *vigas* to hold up the ceiling, and a wooden floor—was to be the Normal School's "signature" building. It took about three years to complete it, with Senator Bronson Cutting bequeathing some money for the school to use as it wished, and President Roosevelt listening to a messaged plea from Joe Grant for money to finish the building.

But they got it done, and it is indeed *the* handsome building on the campus.

◻

Joe Grant, besides building the campus, performed another magnificent deed. He built an ambient in which students could feel that they belonged. Students acquired self-confidence in their worth and their ability to function in life with other people. He did this by showing great loyalty to staff, and incorporating students and graduates, former Children of the Normal School, into his staff.

The presidency of a school or college offers as many opportunities for failure as it does for success, however. This president, and several in the Normal School's future, failed in a couple of important ways. Grant was unable to overcome what is commonly called the "town and gown" problem. He did not open the campus to the community, except to those who worked at the school. This meant that the day students were not received with open arms, either. Elementary school children remained someone else's responsibility, eventully the county's charge.

I have heard the laments of my fellow students from El Rito—sometimes bitter complaints—that they were not received on a par with boarding students as a result of many years of neglectful practices by the Normal School. One of the more obvious reasons was the overwhelming care and concern that was shown for girls who boarded on campus. They were given opportunity to socialize only briefly outside of school hours. The same was not true for boys, who were allowed considerably greater freedom. All of this meant, however, that some segregation of students was viewed as the normal routine of student life.

On the other hand, local students did participate and compete well in organized activities, the school band and athletics, for example. It was in social events that students from El Rito were excluded. A good part of the campus, then, was viewed as off-limits for day students.

In summary, those in charge should have sought a better way.

◻

In the absence of records, or handy evidence that someone tried to chronicle the lives of Children of the Normal School, I sought leads concerning personalities during the differing periods of the Normal School.

Even as late as the mid-1950s when I was there, older students at El Rito would mention Gilbert Archuleta, class of 1934. One of the reasons was that Gilbert maintained an association with the Normal School and Joe Grant for some years after he graduated from the high school. There was a lot more to this, however. Gilbert Archuleta was one of the most gifted athletes in northern New Mexico to come along in a generation.

Gilbert played basketball, as did most good athletes. The Eagles were lucky to have a gym—small as a cracker box—in which one ten-second line was a foot or two beyond the top of the key, and the same thing once one crossed the line on the opponents' court. Walls were almost touching each of the out-of-bounds lines. But, no matter. Kids were glad to have their gym, the only one for at least thirty miles around.

It was in baseball that Gilbert Archuleta made his mark and for which some people still remember him. Joe Grant followed the boy's fortunes while in high school, and Joe, who had played semi-pro ball in New York and California, knew when he had a real player on his hands. After graduating, Gilbert took a job coaching at the school, but in 1939 he announced to the Board of Regents that he was likely to be drafted to play in organized baseball. Joe Grant beamed as Gilbert made this known; Grant guessed that Gilbert Archuleta had a bright future in baseball, as a pitcher.

According to Carlos Salazar, sports editor for the old *Albuquerque Tribune*, in 1939 Branch Rickey of the St. Louis Cardinals made "a special trip to Albuquerque on the Santa Fé Chief" to sign Gilbert Archuleta to a contract. That summer of 1939 he posted a record of 11 wins and two losses for the Albuquerque Cardinals of the Arizona-Texas League. Gilbert moved up to Pocatello and Sacramento in the farm system, but in 1942 he joined the Navy in response to the Japanese attack on Pearl Harbor. With the Seabees in Guadalcanal, he played ball against a couple of guys named Dominic Dimaggio and Phil Rizutto, who became New York Yankees after the war.

As happened to several young men, World War II took their best years; Gilbert Archuleta, who could have excelled on the ball field, was one of them.

Gilbert Archuleta came home at the advanced age of 30 to play for the Albuquerque Dukes in the old West Texas-New Mexico League. Again, he won eleven and lost two games the first summer, and then in 1947 he won 17 games without a loss at Tingley Field.

Gilbert's pitching career was for all practical purposes over, however, having secured a good job with the New Mexico Employment Security Commission. My understanding is that Gilbert pitched for the Dukes for sixty bucks a game toward the end of his career, a real deal for the Albuquerque Dukes.

Down the road from my home in Española lives another former baseball great, in our parts, Rubén Archuleta, Gilbert's younger brother. Rubén has spoken with me about his brother and given me the leads I have needed to examine what record there is of Gilbert's life. Wish that Rubén would talk with me about himself that way, but he hasn't. Other Children of the Normal School have told me about him. We'll be seeing him again in this story.

回

Cloide Trujillo, now in her mid-nineties, is loved by former students who knew her at El Rito. She is one of the Children of the Normal School herself, although when I first knew her in 1953 she was in charge of about five people at the school's laundry. She had held several positions at the Normal School, including that of chef and girls' dormitory advisor.

Cloide was the person to know if you needed cheering up; she still is. She is like many of the kids who came to El Rito, but she tells the story about her experiences there better than just about anyone. Cloide speaks to the joy of life, even when times have been tough.

She was born Cleofas Herrera in Blanco, New Mexico in April 1917. She was named after her grandfather. Her father was Telefor. Cloide lost her mother at a very young age, but she managed to remain in Blanco and started at the Catholic school at Santa Rosa de Lima Church with Ursuline sisters.

She spoke about growing up on the edge of Navajo country in Blanco. If you do not know or cannot recall, Blanco is almost halfway between the Navajo and Jicarilla Apache Nations. Cloide beamed as she recalled a young friend whose parents herded sheep and goats as their livelihood. She remembered the hogan where her friends lived, and recalled those childhood days as pleasant times.

Cloide's grandma, Anastacíta Valdez, and aunt Teresíta helped her growing up. Young Cleofas showed an aptitude for math, geometry, and languages, and she was a good speller. Her aunt and uncle Fernando saw her potential and brought her from Blanco to El Rito and the Normal School to board as a student.

Cloide was homesick for a brief while, but she made friends and began to excel playing basketball. By this time, late 1920s, the gym was ready and Cloide joined the basketball team, then coached by Father Bikhaus. The good father was parish priest down the road in

El Rito at the church of San Juan Nepomuceno and he volunteered to help with the girls' team.

Cloide told me a surprising story, about which she laughed as she told me the incident. Toward the end of one game, she was closely guarded—too close, maybe—and in self defense she threw the ball backward and up and, sure enough, the ball—swish!—fell through the hoop.

Cloide grew up to be a young woman at the campus of the Normal School, where now in eleventh grade, she met a quiet fellow who was working in maintaining those beautiful grounds before he left town in search of a better job. Abe Trujillo, her future husband, went to work for the New Mexico Highway Department for a brief while, but he decided there were better paying jobs in the ship yards in San Francisco. Besides, it afforded the opportunity to see another part of these United States.

Abe returned to El Rito in order to marry Cloide; Father Bikhaus married the couple in 1936. Not too long after this, Abe was drafted into the US Army and shipped off to Okinawa.

Cloide consoled herself as best she could and decided that the best way to occupy her time was to start an employment career of her own. At times she worked at the Normal School, and other times at the US Post Office. After the war, she and Abe, who is now deceased, settled in El Rito with their family: daughters Olivia, Eva, Paula, and Anna Marie; sons David, Herman, Alfonso, Benjamin, and Patrick.

I remember well some of Cloide and Abe's children at El Rito from our days at the Normal School. David and Olivia were students, as was their younger brother Herman, in elementary school. Years later Herman would become my boss as a Regent on the Board of Northern New Mexico Community College.

◙

Dana and Jewell Allison, brother and sister, came to the Normal School about 1936 when their parents moved to Canjilón from Oklahoma. Dana remembered that he started school in fourth grade. He did not complete high school; he left after eleventh grade to take a job, not at all uncommon for the Children of the Normal School, boys in particular. Jewell completed high school and graduated with the class of 1939.

In gathering information for this book, I was anxious because the class of 1939 was one of the lists of students that I did not have. I have not met Jewell to this day, but Katie Bateman, her sister-in-law, got in touch with Jewell and then e-mailed the list to me. Contrast this ease of communication in this early 21st century with the Normal School's isolation prior to about 1940.

Like many young men at the Normal School, Dana's first love was basketball. He played on the starting five in 1941, 1942, and 1943. Charlie Brown, since deceased, but whom I met about 1978, was Dana's basketball coach.

The Normal School Eagles had several successful seasons during Dana's time at the school. Rivalries existed with large and small schools alike: Santa Fe, Española, and Las Vegas High School, but also St. Catherine's and other small schools. Dana, always a good defensive player and playmaker, became the Eagles' top scorer in his final year at the Normal School.

Dana married Katie Bateman, daughter of Olive Parker, all of them originally from Canjilón and El Rito.

🔲

Alonzo Vigil, class of 1938, is best remembered by students of the 1940s and 1950s as coach and boys' dorm proctor. Alonzo, two brothers, Paul and Pat, and a sister Laura, all graduated at the Normal School; they were Albuquerque kids. A younger brother Billy also attended the Normal School, to grade eleven.

Al Vigil was a service veteran, and one of Joe Grant's favorite people. Alonzo was one of the staff, and former Child of the Normal School, who remained to work through the influence of Joe Grant. Alonzo remained at the Normal School until 1951, when Joe Grant resigned, then returned to the school in 1956. I knew him during my final year at the Normal School.

For Al, who chose to stay at the Normal School, it seemed that its allure never ended. Al Vigil could have made a career in home construction, or a similar field. He was particularly good at working with wood. One day I was sitting at the home of Pat Vigil and was admiring a dining room set done in Spanish Colonial style. Pat said, "Guess for a minute who made it." It turned out to be one of Al's fine work. It was a skill, of course, learned by guys like Al at the Normal School.

Pat referred to his brother Al as "one of the kindest people" whom he has known. I know, I know, Pat and Al were brothers, and it's what you'd expect Pat to say. But this is a statement that I have heard over and over made by students about another of the Children of the Normal School.

◻

John Martin is of the class of 1939. According to John, the Martin family returned to stay in El Rito in 1923. John was eight months old. If I were to suggest to someone back east, who'd never been west of the Ohio, that he should meet some of my neighbors, John would be among three or four who would come to mind immediately. John is fluent in Spanish, having grown up in El Rito, and began his formal education at the Normal School. Moreover, he is warm, gentlemanly, and tells some of the funniest stories I've heard.

Now in his late eighties, he remembers El Rito as a quiet place, with very few cars around. Somehow his family got ahold of a 1927 Buick, but he told me the family didn't have much money. His mother and father, however, did not let on to his brothers and sister that they were poor. His father quickly became established in business and managed a modest existence with the family. John and his brothers eventually attended the Normal School. John started in 1929; his first teacher was none other than Laura Redman Dougherty. John is one of the children in a photograph of the first grade class of 1929, in our book.

I have spoken at length with John about growing up during the Great Depression; I missed it, having come along later in 1940. John's impressions are similar to my own parents', who simply considered that this was a most dreadful period in our United States. They witnessed countrymen in abject poverty and dire need.

John gives me the impression that this singular event left him a humble man, and someone resolved to be a good person. For years, when I was president of Northern New Mexico Community College, trying to raise money for students' scholarships via the College Foundation, John served as member of our Foundation Board. I knew John as a man waiting to be asked to join in an effort that would help present and future students in this region to pay for their education.

John told me about the Civilian Conservation Corps, which built roads to Canjilón and La Madera during those depression years. In the thirties, still, El Rito remained isolated: no good roads, no electricity, and no telephones. English was not spoken much in our communities, so John learned Spanish.

The number of men who left El Rito during World War I were few, compared to a later period when more men participated in the Second World War, were what John recalled.

John Conway was president of the Normal School when John started school. He told me Conway hired good teachers, including Laura Dougherty, Barbara Sena, and Carson Creecy. He said that the majority of high school students during all of his time were academic, rather than vocational, students.

When John graduated from high school in 1939, he stayed in El Rito and took courses made available through the college division. Courses were the same ones that had served to train teachers since the late twenties. John found some use in this kind of education, although he would never teach formally. In any case, John's family couldn't afford to send him to college. Brother George was enrolled at Regis College in Denver, which was a sufficiently large expense for the Martins already.

The Second World War was the event that *really* affected this generation of students at the Normal School. John was drafted into the US Army in October 1942, and so he joined many young people from northern New Mexico in the service of country.

John spoke with me about the changed way of life caused by

the war. The economy was improving slightly, but meat and all food and gasoline were rationed. Regarding the same discussion, minutes of meetings of the Board of Regents dealt frequently with the need for administration to budget to buy provisions for the kitchen when certain groceries became available. The Normal School had to be ready to seize opportunity to purchase items as they became available, such being the uncertainty with regard to the availability of rations.

After the war in 1946, John enrolled at the University of New Mexico. Many other returnees from the war were going to California to find jobs. Some did not, and they returned to El Rito. John studied business and Spanish while at UNM. Spanish was his first love, and the combination, in fact, served him well in his professional life.

George and John earned BA degrees and set out for the world. John was recalled by the US Army during the Korean War, and was commissioned a second lieutenant..

His brothers Tom and Pat stayed in El Rito. Tom ran the store and Pat became a rancher.

John Martin made a career in banking and worked with the US Agency for International Development in El Salvador. He lives in Santa Fé with his wife Barbara, whom he married in December 1951. They have two sons, Meade and Christopher.

▣

After the shakeup of the administration in 1934, and announcement of the school's intention to emphasize vocational studies, Joe Grant quietly created what came to be called the "college division." He had been receiving welcome advice concerning the academic program, and he accepted the idea that the Spanish American Normal School should continue to try to train teachers for the schools in this region.

Among those individuals whom he hired to guide the school in this direction were Herbert W. Prather, James A. McNeil, and W.D. Caster, who each served as principal of the high school in the order mentioned. The man hired to head the college division was Charles H. Robinson, who was to play an important role in the school almost twenty years later. Robinson is one of the real heroes in this story, and he merits attention again, later in this book.

Howard Sylvester, whom I knew as a language professor in later years at New Mexico Tech, was another individual who headed the college division for a brief while.

□

Lives of people in northern New Mexico were only slightly changed in spite of the looming war, which didn't really begin until early in the next decade for the United States. The Great Depression had been awful, leaving people shaken and their confidence scarred, sometimes for the remainder of their lives. The Children of the Normal School had been somewhat more secure in their environment. Joe Grant had built a nice campus for them, and those who resided on the campus knew how much better life was at the Normal School than in many of our communities.

By January 1940, the campus was complete with the exception of two major buildings added more than a dozen years later. Minor construction is a way of life on most campuses, and it continued to be at the Normal School.

6

THE NORMAL SCHOOL'S BEST DECADE, the forties, was also its saddest because of forces totally out of its control. Why would we consider it its finest decade? To begin, the campus was complete; construction, the movement of men and building materials, stopped. The school acquired a telephone; other comforts that affected students had long been installed and the school functioned as a modern campus. There was water on campus, heavily treated perhaps, because its quality was seldom the best. Electricity was provided, at least intermittently, with the school's own generator. But the beauty of the campus was what was most evident, as trees and plants grew and matured. The students' school newspaper, *El Aguila*, would now and again carry a brief essay pointing to the natural beauty of the campus.

◻

Youngsters from El Rito were still very uneasy about the welcome accorded them—or better said, barely accorded them—on campus. Some of our more vocal contemporaries may be heard still decrying this very matter, because this situation was real, seldom imagined. But they bore the burden of initiating relations and making friends with other kids on campus, in the hope that their circumstances would get better. And occasionally they did. Some individuals were always wonderful, and they made up, on occasion, for other snubs that day students felt.

◻

Jane Goddard, who was known as Jane García after she married, finished school at El Rito the year before she was listed as graduating, 1940. Jane grew up in El Rito with her father and mother. Jane learned English at home, her father did not speak Spanish; her mother , a woman from Roswell originally, spoke the beautiful Spanish spoken in Mexico, but Jane learned from a neighboring girl and spoke our local Spanish.

Jane started school in 1929 with Laura Redman Dougherty. She too is in a photograph I have included in this book of the first grade class of 1929. Jane later had classes with Cecilia de Baca Redman and Barbara Sena. In high school she had a teacher, Josué Trujillo, whom she admired.

Jane was an avid reader and the library of the Normal School had many, many books from which to choose. She enjoyed the education that she received and thought it quite good. She complained to me, mostly on behalf of her contemporaries from El Rito, that the Normal School showed little regard for day students. There were no activities for them to attend; not even a place for the kids to have lunch was designated on campus. She stopped going to ball games because other social activities, such as school dances, were off limits to students from El Rito. She did not think that the kids from El Rito had a good feeling about the school, as a result of this negligence on the part of management. She was referring here to the late thirties and early forties, Joe Grant's years.

Jane married Fabián García in 1941. Fabián had attended St. Michael's High School in Santa Fé. They had ten children, most of whom I know. Jane and Fabián had an acquaintance with each of the presidents of the Normal School, very positive ones from what I know.

Jane's parents lived in El Rito until her mother Augusta died in 1945 and Clarence in 1951. Fabián her husband passed away in January 2005.

Jane and Fabián were excellent neighbors of the Normal School, exceptionally friendly and helpful, all the time that my wife Angela and I resided on campus.

▣

Many of the Children of the Normal School of the thirties are no longer of this earth, and there were many more, some still living, than I have included in this brief story. Lists of names of some classes in the

1930s may be found in the Appendix. With the decade of the forties, maintaining track of students who started at the school, and those who finished, became complicated by the onset of war, World War II. The lists of graduating classes of the 1940s, however, tend to be complete for the most part.

□

Readers may recall that Japan attacked Pearl Harbor on December 7, 1941 and President Roosevelt immediately convened the Senate of the United States and declared war the following day. Four days later, Adolf Hitler declared Germany's war on the United States, and a war that had been on the European continent since 1939 finally engaged this country.

Young men who graduated between 1939 to 1942 became targets of the military draft. Children of the Normal School attending in 1943 and 1944 were inducted into the armed services either while they were still in school or immediately upon graduation. After a while, our soldiers seemed younger and younger.

The war in Europe, via England, then Normandy and Belgium, required lots of soldiers in order to capture Germany and Berlin, their ultimate objectives.

In the Pacific Islands, war with Japan became a bitter conflict. War on two fronts depleted the population of young men of the USA, clearly evident in the student population on the campus of the Spanish American Normal School.

In September 1943, school President Joseph B. Grant addressed remarks to students that were reported in *El Aguila*. He started by saying that students should expect some loss of privilege and advantages that they had enjoyed at the Normal School heretofore. He pointed to the bravery of the young people who had departed to war. But he ended with a poignant statement: "I know that you all join in a prayer for the return of our former students and all those connected with our cause, and for those who have already made the supreme sacrifices, and now lie sleeping in a foreign land, let us pray that they may have found peace with their God, knowing that they died for us and that we will never betray those ideals for which they gave all."

Very soon during that fall term, the football season of the Normal School had to be canceled. There were an insufficient number of boys to constitute a team.

Students' anxiety showed in words published also in *El Aguila*. With regard to Armistice Day, 1943, a holiday that had been declared commemorating the end of World War I, the paper ended with the observation that, "This day has been declared a holiday. Today we face the same problem, or even a greater one, but we sincerely hope that again the axis powers will be vanquished. Let us pray for a quick victory." These were powerful words written during a desperate time by Alfonso Luján, the assistant editor.

◙

Gordon Darling, who graduated in 1943, followed a somewhat more circuitous route than most students from beginning to end at the Normal School.

I met Gordon during a large reunion of the Children of the Normal School in 1998 on the campus at El Rito. I was impressed with his accomplishments as a grown man, and touched by his expression of love for the school and for Joe Grant, in particular.

Gordon was a very young boy when he came to El Rito, the first time. He had started school in Estancia, in first grade in 1932, but two years later, he was brought to the Spanish American Normal School. Gordon felt picked on by older boys who even tried to molest him, and in his memoirs, which he allowed me to read, he states that, when an opportunity occurred, he "ran away." He spent the mid-thirties in Albuquerque and in Stanley. His mother brought him back to El Rito in 1938; Gordon wondered why she would do that.

Gordon's new circumstances at the Normal School turned out to be entirely different from the first time. Joe Grant paid special attention to him and made certain that he was comfortable. Luckily for Gordon that he had found his new home; his mother died, a victim of an automobile the following year, in 1939.

Gordon met new people, including Rubén Miera and Pat

Martin, who became his best friends. He also became involved in sports with coach Charlie Brown.

Gordon provided me with written observations about the Normal School as it was between 1938 and 1943. He summarized, "Most impressive was El Rito's *esprit de corps*. To be associated with El Rito Normal School meant belonging to a community stressing caring, culture, sharing, pride and achievement and reaching one's full potential."

Gordon was president of the class of 1943, and in parting he thanked the faculty and President Joe Grant for "for all they have done for us."

Gordon loved New Mexico, felt confident of his belonging here, and felt that if he would of stayed he may have become US senator or governor of the state or president of the school.

His leadership in civic organizations, during his adult life, has been recognized in documents and newspapers in the Nation. One of the several awards Gordon has received that is particularly impressive is the Roberto Clemente Humanitarian Award for his twenty-five years of service in Vallejo, where he lived in California.

▣

Rubén Miera is a well-known political figure in New Mexico, and friend to many of us. He is also of the class of 1943.

When Rubén started school in Sandoval County, the public high school in Bernalillo "barely existed," as he remembered. Our Lady of Sorrows, the Catholic school, was better known. Rubén was interested in athletics, however, and El Rito seemed the place to be. Once he arrived at the Normal School, Rubén played football for Charlie Brown's teams, and he turned out to be a good running back.

Parenthetically, I should mention that we youngsters were known often by English and Spanish names, sometimes interchangeably. As the Spanish name, we place the accent over Rubén's name; in English, we don't.

Rubén told me his days at El Rito were "the happiest days I ever had. We lived like brothers and sisters." Rubén was particularly reliable in this way; he shared his money with schoolmates, because other kids didn't have very much. He loved the place. After he graduated, for a time he visited El Rito often.

After graduation, Rubén managed to survive the war years by serving as a dental technician in the US Navy. Upon his return to New Mexico he operated a store and bar in Algodones, his old home. He told me that US Senator Joseph Montoya at one point promised Rubén that he would "make a politician out of you." He did, readily. Rubén served as *de facto* chairman of the Democratic Party in Sandoval County for about fifty years, finally becoming the elected head of the party in 1955.

Ruben Miera, the public figure, has served in various elected and appointed offices in state government. He served in both administrations of Governors Bruce King and Jerry Apodaca, as Secretary of Transportation. Other times, he has served as Assistant State Auditor, State Auditor, and Assistant Secretary of State.

Rubén became widowed and remarried; he lives in Algodones.

◻

Pat Martin was also a member of the class of 1943.

He was the youngest of five children of first-President George J. Martin and Margaret Allen Martin, having been born Patrick O. Martin in July 1923.

Pat Martin attended elementary school in El Rito, then enrolled at the Normal School for high school. He was a popular student, not least for his musicianship. Pat participated with the *Orquesta Típica* founded by an enthusiastic young teacher named Pablo Mares.

The *Orquesta Típica* was composed principally of singers and strings, violins, guitars, an occasional *guitarrón* or bass. The orchestra played folkloric pieces, some of ancient Spanish or Mexican origin, all of it to appreciative audiences. They played far and wide in New Mexico, including the Lensic Theater in Santa Fe, venues in Albuquerque, and I saw one advertisement for the *Orquesta* performing in the Carlsbad Caverns.

After graduation, Pat remained on the ranch. He had a military deferment because he was the only son in the Martin family on the ranch to do the work. When John came home in 1946, Pat was drafted into the US Army.

Pat attended the University of New Mexico one semester. He quickly resumed life ranching in El Rito. He married Joann Severns in the mid-fifties. The Martins had two boys, Mike and Timothy.

Pat was one of a few full time ranchers left, a *real* cowboy. His sons followed in his steps.

Joann Martin, his wife, was a teacher who took an interest in creation of the new school district that was designated to replace the Normal School, a story we'll examine later in this book. The community had to get ready for the eventuality; she assisted with that.

Pat became a member of the New Mexico Cattle Growers and was the Cattle Inspector for the Livestock Board at one time. He was a founding member of the El Rito Fire Department, located across the road from the Normal School campus.

Mike Martin, Pat's older son, was a member of the Board of Regents of Northern New Mexico Community College, appointed by Governor Garrey Carruthers, during one of my presidencies at the community college.

Pat Martin passed away in February 1976. Tim, the Martin's younger son, died in June 2006. Father and son were both known for their pleasant disposition and for their work ethic, reliability, and neighborliness.

◎

Paul Romero graduated from the Normal School in spring 1944.

The Second World War affected profoundly Paul's view of the world. I interviewed this fine, sensitive man in his home in Albuquerque, after I learned that he had graduated with the class of 1944 and that he had served with the US Army immediately following.

Paul Romero, from Velarde, came to El Rito to finish high school. Paul's father *don* Flavio and his mother *doña* Cirila wanted him to have a better education than he was receiving in the valley, and they encouraged him to attend the Normal School. His mother was a teacher who taught in rural schools in Lyden, La Canova, and Velarde. She was known as *la maestra.*

Paul's soon-to-be fiancée was Cecilia Valdez, a young woman also from Velarde. Cecilia was studying to be a teacher. Paul remembered that she was one of only two students enrolled in the college division.

Paul and Cecilia were to be married following high school, but the threat of the war caused him to counsel her that they had best await the outcome of the war. World War II "disturbed everything" is how Paul describes what occurred to young people of the time. As we spoke, it occurred to me that his happy memory of El Rito was overshadowed by flashbacks of the war.

Paul Romero was an infantryman. He said to me, "Recall that General McArthur is remembered for saying to the people of the Philippine Islands, 'I shall return.'" Well, Paul told me, he did, on the backs of US Army infantrymen who retook Luzon and the capital, Manila, inch by inch because the Japanese would not surrender the battle. Paul remembered people rejoicing as the war ended in August 1945. Paul and his infantry buddies were still on Luzon.

Paul hated to see the savagery that people bring on each other during war. He told me that he hoped that people here would never see the destruction that war causes, and the abject poverty and disease following war. He said these things to me with sadness and barely veiled anger. But he never spoke about himself without my urging.

Following the capture of the Philippines, Paul and other seasoned soldiers were sent to occupy Korea, which had also been liberated from Japan. He witnessed the creation of the 38th parallel by which Korea was divided north and south. North Korea was pro-Soviet, and South Korea became a durable ally of the United States.

Paul was discharged from the Army in September 1946. He and Cecilia were married the following April in Velarde. I participated in their wedding as the small boy who carried wedding rings for the bride, who was my grand aunt, and my new uncle.

Paul and Cecilia had children Paul, Larry, Geraldine, James, Ann, Carmela, and Barbara.

Cecilia Valdez Romero died in October 2001; Paul lives in Albuquerque.

◙

Ted Kuntz graduated with the class of 1946.

He was a boy from Farmington whose father worked on construction projects wherever he could find work. Ted and his dad met Earl Scarborough, who suggested he might like the school at El Rito. Ted came to the Normal School at age eleven. I have included Ted's picture with other students in woodworking classes. Vocational classes were important to a good number of the Children of the Normal School.

When I asked Ted what he had profited from most at the Normal School, I found his answer interesting. His response: "The school taught me to be independent and to think." Ted's statement seems to be an underlying theme in many of these discussions with former students.

Ted's recollection about the war, and how it affected him, has a happier ending than most I heard. Ted went into the US Navy after high school, and was on the way to the South Pacific when his ship was told to return home. The war had ended and our boys were no longer needed in that vast expanse beyond Hawaii.

◙

The paucity of information at the Normal School about veterans of the Second World War is enough to sadden anyone. Allusions to the war, which I have referred to in *El Aguila*, are general statements decrying the war and its hardships, but there is little mention of specific individuals and their deeds or circumstances. One of the reasons was that the Normal School did not have a student yearbook then, or anything similar. No formal means of commemorating its heroes existed. Nor was there a record of casualties of soldiers who had been students at the school. After the school ceased to operate as a high school, there were few records left in any one place of students who had attended the Normal School. What the reader will find in the Appendices, I put together from scattered sources.

◙

Ross López graduated with the class of 1947.

Ross, from Española, decided late in his high school career to attend El Rito. His brief year at the Normal School resulted in a loyal alumnus of the school, whose many friends include his old schoolmates. That kind of familial environment is what appealed to Ross.

I mentioned to Ross my concern about the little information that I had run across concerning World War II veterans who had been Children of the Normal School. Ross pointed to a photograph in the 1947 *El Chamisal*. The caption states in all capital letters "VETERANS BASKETBALL TEAM." Players names are listed: Eliseo Baca, Elfego Aranda, Dan Lovato, Ross López, Celestino Jaramillo, Manager Salomon Archuleta, Samuel Romero, Miqueas Girón, Ernest Gurulé, Albert Ulibarrí, and Coach Al Vigl. Team players had uniforms that said "El Rito."

Ross explained to me. He was not a veteran, but as a transfer student he was ineligible by interscholastic rules to play for the varsity Eagles. Al Vigil suggested that he join veterans on their team.

Years later, sometime in fall 2010, Ross López invited us to a luncheon at Rancho de Chimayó attended also by Ernesto Gurulé, Elías Montoya, Élfego Aranda, Reyes Gonzáles, and Leo Apodaca. Dennis Salazar and I were the younger members in the group. This illustrates, better than words can, the enduring camaraderie among Ross and his friends.

Ross and his wife Lydia live in Española.

◙

The classes of 1947 and 1948 for a long time have constituted a group of former students who have remained in contact with each other and who have enjoyed meeting frequently.

A couple of members of their group, John Aragón and Anna Mae King, were sometimes referred to as guardian angels. When they were Children of the Normal School, John and Anna Mae were leaders; as the years progressed, they continued to call their friends together.

The class of 1947 was larger than most at the Normal School: 51. The class of 1948 was smaller: 35. I knew more than a dozen of them fairly well, thanks in great measure to John Aragón with whom I worked several years at Highlands and in Latin America.

In observing these former students of the late 1940s, I have come to believe that the Normal School reached its zenith during this period. The ambience about which they speak, the zeal with which they describe plays, "follies," ball games, and their social life are delightful, their laughter and banter mesmerizing.

I have known of more and better—certainly better funded—boarding schools in England and in New England, USA. But as you read their students' comments, reactions to the institutions are mixed. The Normal School of the forties, especially, seems to have left a memory with each student akin to a fond dream.

◻

During the 1947–1948 school year an action of the President of the Normal School and the Board of Regents was taken quietly, and only by year's end was it made widely known. After almost forty years, they elected to call the school at El Rito Northern New Mexico Normal School, a name more apt for a school that had been serving a wider population than Spanish American students. Particularly among students, the name change was welcomed.

Someone determined that the Eagles' fight song would be the "The Stars and Stripes Forever," written by John Philip Sousa. The patriotic song may have been adopted earlier in the history of the school. Sousa lived almost half of the nineteenth century, and well into the twentieth, expiring in 1932. All that we have is a recollection of the tune and its use of "NNMNS" in its newly assigned lyrics.

◻

Leo Apodaca, class of 1947 spoke to me for this book. I had known Leo as a classmate of John Aragón, but have gotten to know him better in recent times. Leo spoke about the basic things that a young man needed in his life to maintain interest in school, and to be comfortable. Everything at El Rito met his needs: the dormitories, dining room, friends, caring teachers and so on. The kids were well fed and felt secure.

Leo was an Albuquerque boy, who seldom missed the city. The sports program at the Normal School kept him plenty busy: football, basketball, and baseball, mostly. Someone stuck him with the name "Sluggo," he chuckled, he didn't mind. Leo smiles and laughs a lot as he recounts days at El Rito.

Leo attended New Mexico Highlands University for training as a teacher, after leaving El Rito. This prepared him for a career in his home town, Albuquerque, where he still lives.

◩

Danny Englebrecht was another Albuquerque boy. Danny had an all-consuming interest in sports. He even tried boxing, and he found that he could be pretty good. Danny speaks in short bursts, as though he were still a young man in training. This group of students to whom Danny belonged were well-conditioned young men.

Danny's mother worked in Albuquerque where she and Danny met Alonzo Vigil, who suggested that he might try the boarding school at El Rito. In 1941, at age 13, Danny enrolled at the Normal School. At El Rito he blossomed, and one year he was state boxing champion as a bantamweight. Danny never missed home, and thereafter he saw Albuquerque as simply a place for a summer job.

Leo, Danny, and Ted were having a discussion about their days at the Normal School. They viewed the Grants as parents, mother and father figure, although they did not see Joe Grant very often. As they agreed, "We were members of one family." They remembered Al Vigil and Charlie Brown with special fondness.

Leo, Danny, and Ted view their individual lives as having been a success, and they got their start on the right path in El Rito.

◩

David Grant was the son of Joe Grant and Anita Segura Grant; he came to the campus a few months after his father was hired as president of the Normal School. David, always a little younger than his classmates, graduated with the class of 1947.

David Grant was a friend of John Aragón, and he'd worked with John at Highlands long after I had left there, so I had not met David. I called him at his home in Albuquerque in summer 1997, because I needed help in planning a reunion of the Children of the Normal School for the following year. David welcomed me, and we spoke mostly about his dad

David helped me to prepare for the reunion in ways that exceeded any expectation that I may have had. He allowed me to borrow home movies that his father had taken at the Normal School in the late thirties and forties. Joe Grant had been president of the Normal School more than seventeen years, and he had documented a lot of it on film, mostly with images of his family and students of the Normal School. A talented cinematographer who was on our staff at the community college, Roger Salles, selected material from each year and created a beautiful film, accompanied by period music like "Moonlight Serenade," written by Glenn Miller about 1935. Needless to say, the film made quite a hit with alumni in attendance the summer of 1998 in El Rito.

David loved his parents, who were no longer living in 1997. But eventually I got him to talk about himself and his recollection of years at the Normal School.

David had two interests as a student. He loved to play basketball, and he was on the team, known as the "midgets," that was favored to win the state championship in 1947. They were knocked out of the state tournament, instead, by tiny St. Catherine's of Santa Fé. The El Rito Eagles included David, Reyes Gonzáles, Buzzy Newbern, John Aragón, Andrés "Casey" Martinez, Pat Vigil, Leo Fernández, Edward Salazar, Leo Montoya, and Danny Englebrecht.

His second interest was photography, especially as applied in journalism. One of his lasting accomplishments at the Normal School was in the publication of the first student yearbook, *El Chamisal*, in 1947. From 1947 on, students managed to continue this popular picture book, from which a number of photos in this book are taken.

David emphasized to me that other activities were as important as sports when he was a student. Pablos Mares gained a reputation in northern New Mexico for the *Orquesta Típica*, and later in his career composed the state song.

He told me about Lena Archuleta, who directed the "Follies," a takeoff on the "Follies Bergere" that was first produced in Paris about 1869. Ms. Archuleta and the students may have learned about the "Follies" from a movie made in the US with the identical title, starring Maurice Chevalier. The "Follies," then, were not about skin, as deterioration of the theme in Europe had led people to expect; the productions were about music and costuming. Elaborate productions. Children of the Normal School who were at El Rito in the late forties have told me—I can't count how many times—about the "Follies."

David remembered fondly some of his teachers and friends: Lena Archuleta, Opel Winfield, Charlie López, Gilbert Archuleta, Wallace Archuleta, and, of course, fellow students John Aragón and Pat Vigil. He told me about a student from El Rito, Norbert Trujillo, whom he described as being "smarter than all of us."

David Grant left the Normal School at a young age, after graduating. He attended an additional year of high school in Santa Fé, then went on to the University of New Mexico, where he took a degree in political science.

In time, David managed the northern branch of the *Albuquerque Journal*. David represented the Ford Foundation in New Mexico for a number of years, and he assisted young scholars in their development by finding them scholarships and interesting projects. He joined the staff of New Mexico Highlands University during the last few years of John Aragón's presidency.

The last time I saw David was during our school reunion in 1998, which he told me he and his younger brother, James, had enjoyed.

David died unexpectedly not long after we had seen him at the alumni's reunion.

▣

Two students from the class of 1948 whom I did not know

well—I probably saw each of them once—were spoken about by their classmates.

Norbert Trujillo was class valedictorian, but in addition to being at the top of his class, fellow students remember him as one of the brightest people whom they knew. Norbert grew up in El Rito, as did a number of other good students. Norbert attended New Mexico State University and studied mathematics. He was employed by the White Sands Missile Range, in his professional life. He is retired and lives in Las Cruces.

◙

Another very popular student was Beau Newbern, now deceased. He was from Santa Fé. John Aragón was very fond of "Buzzy,", a fine basketball player. Other students tell me that he was the top player in the district during his final year at the Normal School.

◙

Chis Jaramillo, also from El Rito, was of the class of 1948.

I knew Chris years after his high school and college years. He was one of my favorite teachers at the Normal School about 1956. He showed interest in his students, and was always willing to engage us in quiet conversation.

He taught the business courses and he did a good job of helping me to develop skill in the use of the typewriter.

I remember that students were always comfortable around Chris Jaramillo. He was quiet most of the time, and a real gentleman. The result was that, when he suggested direction for students, they were apt to follow it.

◙

John Aragón was well liked by his schoolmates at the Normal School, and he became one of its prominent alumni.

John prided himself in referring to home as the Barelas district in Albuquerque, although he also had roots in rural San Miguel County.

I met John Aragón in Tegucigalpa, Honduras in 1963. John

was on a visit at the University of Honduras for the Ford Foundation, reviewing projects sponsored by the agency. I was teaching at the same university on a Fulbright lectureship. We were there primarily because of our enthusiasm for President John F. Kennedy's Alliance for Progress, a project designed to assist Latin America in education and economic development.

During this time, John was working on a doctoral degree at the University of New Mexico, under the direction of Frank Angel, a professor in the college of education, and a mutual friend.

Shortly thereafter, John Aragón was appointed executive secretary for the New Mexico School Boards Association, and after completion of his doctoral studies, he took a job at the University of New Mexico as director of the Cultural Awareness Center. He also taught in the college of education.

During the late 1960s and early 1970s, I got to know John well. He was a great story teller and he spoke about people back at the Normal School in his high school days, most of whom I did not know: Anna Mae King, Buzzy Newbern, Norberto Trujillo, Pat Vigil, Tony García, Richard Malooley, David Grant, Carl Naranjo, Joan Odom, Gillie López, Ernest Dow, Leo Sánchez, Andrés "Casey" Martínez, Rubén Archuleta, and many more whom I cannot remember. John loved the people about whom he spoke, and they became larger than life in his telling. John was the first person to tell me about the "Follies" and Lena Archuleta, their teacher.

In the mid-sixties, John became chief of party in Quito, Ecuador in a project sponsored by the federal government in partnership with the University of New Mexico. The University operated a studies center in Ecuador, and it provided technical services to the country's ministry of education. This assignment in Ecuador, providing him with memories which he cherished, was sandwiched in among other assignments that John had with UNM.

In about 1976, John became president of New Mexico Highlands University; this is when I came to know John well. I was the academic dean when John arrived, and he asked whether I would remain in the position. I did, and enjoyed working with John, but in 1979 I resigned the position to come to Northern New Mexico Community College.

John and I remained close friends and professional associates. We worked together on several projects in Guatemala. John was in his heart a latin americanist, and he spoke with enthusiasm about friends and acquaintances in the region.

John was married to Jean Maurice about 1951, during the couples' last year at Highlands University as students. John and Jean Aragón had four children: John, Allison, Lisa, and Joel.

John's health began to fail in late 1976. A week before he died, a group of friends hosted a reunion at the Sheraton Hotel in Albuquerque to pay tribute to a man who had achieved prominence as an educator, and whose presence among us we had so much enjoyed.

John Aragón died in Albuquerque in February 1997.

◨

Anna Mae King graduated from the Normal School in 1948.

Her name entered often in discussion among students of this period. I spoke with her on the telephone for this book. She was as friendly as her classmates had described her to me, cheerful and willing to talk, but she told me that I seemed to have most of the information that she could give me.

Anna Mae King was very popular with schoolmates. She was a student leader, and cheerleader for the sports' teams, but it became clear from discussions that she and her classmates were worldly, more aware of a world outside the Normal School.

Anna Mae was proud of her involvement in the "Follies" and their presentation in her hometown, Santa Fé, in the Lensic Theater. I gathered that there had been other venues for this musical, also.

I was reminded, as I spoke with former students about the "Follies," that they had been popularized again, beginning in 1946, by a production that commemorated the "Ziegfeld Follies," done on Broadway in the early part of the century. The movie, starring Judy Garland and Fred Astair, had one of the longest runs of a musical motion picture in the US. No doubt this lent further impetus to Children of the Normal School to create productions that they would forever carry in their memory.

▣

The presence of new people, particularly teachers, at the Normal School had opened up the outside world for its students. Lena Lovato Archuleta, who came to El Rito as a young teacher and married Wallace Archuleta whom she met on the campus, stayed long enough to influence Children of the Normal School of those years.

Lena Archuleta provided students new avenues for their musical talent. From the more traditional music of the early forties, with its emphasis on Hispanic folklore, Lena took students to more contemporary and popular means of musical expression. Lena Archuleta was the sponsor and director of the "Follies."

Dennis Salazar called me on the phone this past spring to tell me that Lena Archuleta had passed away in Denver.

▣

Pat Vigil, class of 1948, was another boy from the *barrio* of Barelas in Albuquerque.

Pat was born in his hometown in May 1929. He attended the West San José Elementary School, where he met John Aragón.

Pat followed his older brothers and sister to El Rito. Pat surmised that his brother Alonzo had probably followed their uncle Lencho García to the Normal School. Pat and John came to El Rito in the same year, in eighth grade.

Pat has an excellent memory, appreciation for history, a deep love of the Normal School at El Rito, and its people. Although basketball was always first among sports, Pat beamed as he spoke to me about the 1946 baseball season at El Rito. This was a year in which the El Rito Eagles captured third place in the state playoffs.

This team merits special mention. As in most of the US in the forties, the smallest schools, rural or not, were expected to compete against the larger city schools. The El Rito Eagles had to have been unusually strong to be able to compete in 1946.

Pat was in tenth grade and played right field. To hear Pat discuss his teammates that year, they were giants. Charlie Brown was their coach.

Music and art were as important to Pat and his classmates as sports. They spoke with the same fervor about the *Orquesta Típica*, the "Follies," and northern New Mexican art and furniture that they reserved for sports.

Another source of pride about which Pat spoke was the girls' basketball team. He gave me a photograph of one of the teams of the late forties.

Pat grew fond of many of the staff for their warmth and camaraderie. One of the photographs that he supplied me with includes Wallace Archuleta, Joe Grant, Alonzo Vigil and Eloy Abeyta, all of them loyal friends.

Pat Vigil attended Highlands University after high school. He and John Aragón, still inseparable, went there together, but Pat had to leave when he was inducted in the US Army. Pat would return to Highlands, later, to complete his studies.

The Army shipped Pat and a classmate, Juan "Pepino" Vigil, to Hawaii for training. It was the time of the Korean War; Pat and Juan Vigil were assigned to the 35th Regimental Combat Team, elite fighting forces. I asked Pat about these elite military teams, and all that he would say, hesitantly, was, "We weren't looking for good conduct medals."

In South Korea, American troops had the assignment of recapturing the peninsula from Chinese forces that had overrun it. His most vivid recollection was "those doggone mountains," and having to lug his machine-gun on his back. Regretfully, he learned early that Juan Vigil had died in battle. Pat was the last New Mexican and friend to have seen Juan.

Pat Vigil is a disabled veteran of the Korean War. As most good soldiers, he speaks of others who fought during the war, friend and foe. He told me a story about a fierce fight with the Chinese against very difficult odds and about the heroism of a Floridian, a "Hispanic guy," who disobeyed orders and refused to retreat while under fire.

Pat received his orders, about a hundred yards from this man, to hold his position; he did. Pat told me that the soldier, whose heroics he admired, kept the sector from collapsing during the battle, and that he killed about 250 Chinese soldiers. The happy part of the story is that the man, whose name Pat did not remember, was awarded the Medal of Honor. Pat said to me, "He gave us a sense of hope and dignity."

Pat came home in 1953 and married Rosalie Manzanares from La Puente. Rosalie was also of the class of 1948. She is deceased.

Pat has lived in Albuquerque since his return from university studies at Highlands.

▣

Tony García is of the class of 1949. Everyone who knew Tony remembers him, but he doesn't say a lot. He told me, "It's the best thing that happened to me. It kept me out of trouble." I suppose that an Albuquerque boy, which he was, might say that. But he is much more than someone who would be in any trouble. Today, he is more athletic than guys thirty years younger. He remained a competitive runner long past age sixty, and he remains young.

Tony went to El Rito with his brother Ralph. Rubén García, an older brother who attended El Rito for two years, died at Clark's Field in Oahu in 1941 during the Japanese attack on Pearl Harbor.

Something Tony didn't tell me was that he had attended Highlands University, played football, and was an all-conference selection.

Tony lives in Albuquerque with his wife Laura, also class of 1949.

▣

The spread of typhoid fever on the campus rocked the faith that the Children of the Normal School had maintained in their school for many years. All of a sudden, in the fall of 1948, the beauty of the campus and tradition were for naught. Students lives were threatened; two boys died of the disease.

Records of the incident are scant. It is still difficult for anyone

75

to describe what happened. It is clear that the water system, precious and cared for though it was, had failed the Normal School. Several students had to go home as a result of this seriously difficult illness. Two of the boys who came together from Albuquerque, Ted Martínez and Richard García, told me their stories. Ted and Richard were among those who were very young at the school, and who became very ill. I have included what they had to say in their biographical sketches.

Nicomedes Sánchez, a youngster from Park View, and Orlando Griego, a boy from Albuquerque, died during this tragic incident.

◙

Having told you of the presence of typhoid fever on campus in the late forties, can easily make one wonder whether this, in fact, was a decade to view with affection. I did not know the two boys whose lives seem to have ended so needlessly. Their lives are commemorated in the school yearbook, *El Chamisal*.

The very presence of very young boarding students lent an added quality, the appearance of home. Many of the boarding students came while still in elementary school, often grades five to eight, and joined boys and girls from El Rito. The Normal School became their home, and their grateful voices remain loud. Seldom does anyone discuss the tragedy of 1948.

The number of kids from Albuquerque and Santa Fe increased several-fold. The presence of these city kids tended to increase the sophistication of the campus, to make it a bit more cosmopolitan.

Modernization is perhaps *the* key word. There was more money, or better said, at last there was some money. Northern New Mexico at last came into a cash economy.

The Normal School had a telephone, or maybe two. State road 554, the road up from US Highway 84, was paved in the years 1946 and 1947.

The Los Alamos Scientific Laboratory, where the atomic bomb was manufactured, was built in the early forties. The Laboratory and its many employees, in turn, created the need for new businesses in the valley and in Santa Fé, providing the first sign of a strengthening economy.

But it was students who changed the mood and ambience of the campus. Their enthusiasm and effusiveness had to have been unmatched in the annals of the Normal School.

Joseph B. Grant became the ninth president of the Normal School in 1934. Design of the campus and many of the present buildings owe to Grant's tenure as president.

This photograph of the campus, looking north, was taken around 1940. Its design is evident, as are the WPA-funded structures that had been completed by this time.

Cutting Hall came into full use about 1937, after strenuous effort by the school to obtain funding for its completion. It was considered the "signature" building at the time, and is more so today. The interior of the small auditorium is, in particular, eye-catching.

The *orquesta típica,* conducted by music instructor Pablo Mares, gained accolades for the school during the mid-1940s.

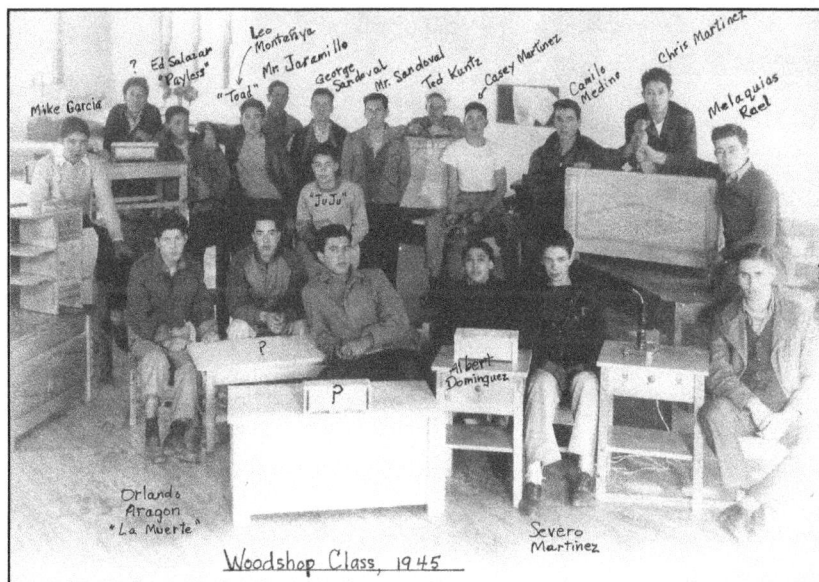

Woodworking is a program of long standing at the Normal School for which the school gained recognition. Items on display are similar to those produced in modern times at Northern New Mexico College. This 1945 photograph has no legend and only an unknown former student's writing to identify his classmates who are, from left to right in the back row, Mike García, unidentified, Ed Salazar, Leo Montaño, Instructor Jaramillo, George Sandoval, Instructor Sandoval, Ted Kuntz, Casey Martínez, Camilo Medina, Chris Martínez, and Melaquías Rael. Orlando Aragón is in front and left. Albert Dominguez and Severo Martínez are fourth and fifth from the left. The remaining students are unidentified.

The El Rito Eagles baseball team in 1946 included Top row: Buzzy Newbern, Frankie Gallegos, Camilo Medina, John Aragón, Ed Salazar, Ruben Archuleta, Leo Montoya, and Rumaldo Miera. Bottom row: Pat Vigil, Henry Martínez, Casey Martínez, Mike García, Leo Fernández, Billie Frank, and Eliseo. Not pictured is Coach Charlie Brown. Photograph is courtesy of Pat Vigil.

The Eagles' veterans basketball team in 1947 included Top row: Manager Salomon Martínez, Samuel Romero, Miqueas Girón, Ernest Gurulé, Albert Ulibarrí, and Coach Al Vigil. Bottom row: Eliseo Baca, Elfego Aranda, Dan Lovato, Ross López, and Celestino Jaramillo. Photograph is from 1947 *El Chamisal*.

Joseph Grant enjoyed friendship with a number of staff. In this picture, taken in 1949, are (left to right) Juan "Wallace" Archuleta, Joe Grant, Alonzo Vigil, and Eloy Abeyta. Photograph is courtesy of Pat Vigil.

Girls at the Normal School began playing basketball competitively in mid-1930s. This picture of the 1947 basketball Eagles includes in Bottom row: Anna Mae King, Mary Mascareñas, Frances García. Middle row: Flora Herrera, Rosina Mendoza, Co-Captain Amelia Baca, Captain Lena Cisneros, Dolores Gómez, Belen Espinoza. Top row: Opal W. Wingfield, Rosella Martínez, Estella Norris, and (not pictured) Gloria Martínez. Photograph is courtesy of Pat Vigil.

This 1948 photograph of students in fifth grade includes in Bottom row: Viola Trujillo, Adonelia Archuleta, Mary Rivera, Arlene Gonzales, Esperanza Baca, Benito Sánchez, and Manuel Martínez. Middle row: Amarante Varoz, Rodolfo Herrera, Cristobal Ocaña, Leroy Velásquez, Peter Trujillo, Valentin Baca, and Carlos Baca. Top row: Virginia Archuleta, Willie Alire, Ben Trujillo, Roberto Ocaña, Ramón Gonzáles, and Alfonso Archuleta.

The grade school Eagles illustrate the young ages at which some of the boarding students arrived at the Normal School. In this 1949 photograph are Front row: Michael Branch, Oscar Saiz, David Borunda, Lupe Juárez, Richard García, and Dennis Salazar. Back row: Joe"Tarzan" Trujillo, Billy Vigil, Eddie Branch, Jimmy Chávez, and Simón Gómez. Not shown is Joe Martinez, team captain.

7

nORTHERN NEW MEXICO NORMAL SCHOOL WAS
VIEWED WITH PRIDE by people of the region, especially by those
who had been its children.

Joe Grant, in addition to being an able manager and politician,
had maintained a steady stream of discussions—mostly one way—with
government, newspapers, and other news outlets about the state of the
Normal School, extolling its benefits to New Mexico. Grant maintained
a reputation as a man who used the resources afforded him to run the
school in a frugal, efficient manner.

The school's administration would receive a sudden jolt soon
after the beginning of the decade, however.

▣

With modernization, the school at El Rito acquired the ability
to attract more, often better, teachers, as the supply increased. Some
of the earlier staff whom Joe Grant had attracted still remained.
Stability that had characterized the Grant years, would suffer and
dissipate, however, as the decade of the fifties would demonstrate.

Children of the Normal School had no inkling of what was
transpiring "behind the scenes," but the signs of change, not for the
better, became increasingly obvious. We'll return to see how a political
drama was played out by its protagonists.

▣

Rubén Archuleta was one of the students who spanned the
late forties and early nineteen-fifties. He graduated with the class of
1950.

Rubén started sixth grade in El Rito in 1942; he was from
Española. Early on, Rubén started to show promise as a baseball

pitcher in little league and junior league. It was about the same time that his brother Gilbert left for the Navy.

At El Rito, Charlie Brown asked Rubén to play high school ball while in eighth grade. By ninth grade, with the confidence of his catcher, "Casey" Martinez, Rubén became a starting pitcher.

Other players told me this, since I would not have been able to pry the story out of Rubén. In spring 1946, at the age of 15, Rubén pitched a no-hitter against the Los Alamos Hilltoppers. Rare though these were anywhere, in northern New Mexico a no-hitter in high school was unheard of.

The baseball Eagles, as Pat Vigil recounted, captured third place in the state tournament, in great part because of this boy pitcher named Rubén Archuleta.

When the school year ended in 1946, Rubén joined the US Army. He was always a tall boy, and even at 15 or 16 he may have looked old enough to officials who inducted him.

In January 1948, Rubén returned to El Rito, looking forward to playing football, baseball, and basketball. *El Chamisal*, 1950, contains a page dedicated to this now grown boy.

Rubén continued building on his local fame as a baseball pitcher, by pitching in summer adult leagues in northern New Mexico. He said to me that he had "only a fastball and counted on good control" for his successes.

I have thought often about how expert coaching could have helped to develop the talents of some of these boys who loved to play ball. For the lack of opportunities, readily available to kids in other parts of the United States, they did not achieve their full potential.

After high school, Rubén went to work for the Los Alamos Scientific Laboratory where he worked from November 1952 until his retirement in June 1986. He and his wife, the former Virginia Montoya, married in January 1953. They have four children: Larry, Marcella, Carlos, and Orlando.

Rubén and Virginia Archuleta reside in Española.

▣

Danny Chávez, Evangeline Manzanares, Evangeline Martínez, and Helen Valdez are of the class of 1951. I do not see some of these former students often, hence I interviewed Helen by telephone.

Evangeline Martínez has been active with the Alumni Association, to whom we owe no small debt of gratitude, for a number of years.

Evangeline Manzanares was class valedictorian; Danny Chávez was salutatorian.

◻

Helen Valdez, class of 1951, was born in 1933; her brother Eli four years later, in 1937. Both Helen and Eli are Children of the Normal School. They have a brother, Ernest, whom I have not met; Ernest attended the Normal School briefly.

Readers met Sixto and Mercedes Valdez, the parents, earlier in this book.

Helen attended the Normal School as a child in sixth grade, seventh, and eighth grades, but when her father took a teaching position in Tierra Amarilla, she attended her middle years of high school in the county seat.

Helen returned to El Rito for grades 11 and 12, then graduated. After high school, she attended Adams State College in Alamosa, Colorado, then transferred to New Mexico Highlands University, where she graduated with a BA degree. She taught elementary school for 28 years in the Española Public Schools.

Helen attended the Normal School by a new name, Northern New Mexico Community College at El Rito, to learn weaving, after her retirement from teaching. She became a very competent weaver, with many of her works displayed throughout New Mexico.

Helen and Ted Bency were married in 1955. Ted is deceased. Helen Bency resides in Los Lunas.

◻

The class of 1952 was unusually small. (To remind the reader, you may find lists of graduating classes in the Appendix.)

Arturo "Casey" Martínez, younger brother of Andrés, was one of the superb athletes of the Normal School, whom people still remember. He was the youngest of three brothers who attended the Normal School. The younger of the Caseys was an unusually strong boy, who played baseball, football, and baskeball, although baseball was by far his sport.

When Casey was in the US Army, he played baseball on a team that included an infielder by the name of Darryl Strickland. Casey could have been a pitcher, but he was drafted by the San Francisco Giants as shortstop, second, and third baseman and he was sent to Giant farm teams. A back injury, suffered while in New England, put a stop to a promising career.

I had known Casey briefly when I was in high school, but we became friends after 1974 when Highlands University recruited him to teach health and physical education and to coach basketball. I was the academic dean, and I learned that Casey had attended universities in his travels, had acquired a BA degree, and then he had received a master's degree from Stanford University. He had some coaching experience in high schools in New Mexico and California. He became a very successful coach at Highlands, and subsequently was named athletic director.

He resigned at Highlands University sometime after I left the institution, and he became superintendent of the Pojoaque school district. After he retired, he lived near Conchas Lake.

Casey Martinez died in December 2003.

◻

Regino Salazar, class of 1952, is one of the students about whom I still hear warm words of praise.

Regino, often called "Reggie," was born in 1933 in Española. Following the premature death of his mother, Regino began attending the Normal School at El Rito at age 13, in eighth grade. Known both for his intelligence and love of sports, he was popular among classmates. Regino was on teams in track, football, baseball, and basketball. In spite of his small size, he was a blocking back on a football team that played the old style single-wing. In baseball, he was a catcher, known among other players for his reliability.

In spite of the great attention that he had devoted to athletics, at graduation in spring 1952, Regino was class valedictorian.

After high school, Regino attended New Mexico Highlands University where he obtained a bachelor's degree in business administration.

In 1957, Regino joined the US Army and he served with his country's occupation forces in South Korea. He continued playing baseball, for an armed services team.

After his hitch in the Army was up, Regino returned to the Española valley to run the family store in El Guache.

Soon after, Regino started making his presence felt in the community as servant, leader, and organizer. He promoted and sponsored, of course, local athletic teams. In 1970, as the result of the appointment of his brother Dennis to the Board of Regents of the New Mexico Technical Vocational School—the old Normal School by its new name—he joined forces with others who believed that the school should expand its new mission, vocational education, to include academic studies.

This is to shorten a very long story. Efforts by Regino Salazar, Dennis Salazar, Regents of the school, local legislators, and the Vocational School's President, Frank Serrano, resulted in the formation of Northern New Mexico Community College. I tell an interesting story that depicts hard work, occasional conflict, considerable intrigue, and local and state politics in another book concerning Northern New Mexico Community College. But Regino, his brother Dennis, and a nucleus of people in the valley were at the center of an effort that was completed satisfactorily.

Many years later, at the turn of the new millennium, Regino organized residents in El Guache, Hernandez, and Española to establish a new water system. Regino Salazar is one of the founders of *Agua Sana* that provides well-water in those communities.

I have spoken with many in the Española valley, and elsewhere, who speak to Regino's good conscience and integrity.

Regino Salazar passed away in November 2005 at age 72.

◻

I met only a few students who graduated in 1953, although I arrived on the campus of the Normal School only a few months after they had finished their last school year.

One student of that time whom I did get to know is Charlie Aragón. When I was in tenth grade, Charlie returned to the Normal School briefly and was placed in charge of the senior boys' dormitory. I remember him as being quiet, very polite, and soft spoken. He was also a good chess player, and he taught me to play.

Charlie came to the Normal School as a young student, preceded by an uncle, Lorenzo "Lencho" García and by his brother John Aragón. Charlie said Lencho was one of the boys who started football at El Rito in the 1930s.

Charlie is a modest guy, but getting him to talk about himself leads you back to the same discussion about his brother John. Charlie is also a thoughtful fellow, however, and this makes it possible to gain rare insights from him about the workings of the Normal School.

Charlie's observations about life at the Normal School during the Joe Grant years had been gained during Grant's final years as president. Charlie had first hand familiarity with the *esprit de corps* that existed there, and which had been described by students ten and fifteen years earlier. He said this was to be seen among students, staff, and teachers, alike. He told me about the profound influence that the departure of Joe Grant from the campus had had on teachers and students alike.

Charlie was also a basketball athlete at El Rito, as you might expect about a boy about six foot three. He was also a good student, and following high school, he went on to the university and became a teacher.

Charlie spent his teaching career with the Albuquerque Public Schools.

◻

Joe Grant had left Northern New Mexico Normal School in

March 1951. Discussions that Charlie was having with me were more than three years later.

The election of November 1950 had resulted in the choice of Edwin L. Mechem as Governor of New Mexico. This was the first time in twenty years that a Republican had occupied the Statehouse. It was *pro forma* for the Board of Regents, who hired the president of the school, to change in favor of the party in power. And it did.

Joe Grant, who understood the method of appointments at the Normal School better than anyone, submitted a friendly and helpful letter of resignation to the Board of Regents in March 1951. He volunteered his services as president to assist the Board in what he hoped would be a brief transition period, and thanked the Board for its consideration in the matter. By summer of the same year, the Board of Regents had hired Edward Medina as its new president.

◙

By 1953, and after two years of an amount of turmoil, Edward Medina had been replaced as president by Clory B. Tafoya.

◙

My first sight of the Northern New Mexico Normal School was in September 1953. I liked it; it brought to mind what a small, high school or college campus should be. It had good ambience. The students seemed happy, given to a bit too much wise-cracking, perhaps, but banter it was. Boys dedicated a fair amount of time in trying to impress one another, and most certainly in attracting girls' attention, but it seemed to me like good, clean fun. The campus was orderly, the buildings were clean, and the outdoors had more shade trees and shrubs than we were used to.

I lived in a dormitory on the second floor of the Junior Building. There were four dorms, with eight beds to a room. We kept our individual spaces orderly, with only a military-style bed and footlocker to worry about. The hall and stairs were well-lit; the one central bath room was clean and seemingly indestructible.

An elderly man, *don* Cruz Jaramillo was our dorm proctor; Lupe Juárez and Dennis Salazar assisted him.

The large influence of teachers and staff at the Normal School on this thirteen-year-old boy was to be long lasting. Because of my interest in science and math, Edward Grant and Glenn George were whom I saw most often. But I also grew fond of Corrine Myers, Chris Jaramillo, Tom Roybal, and our school principal, Facundo Rodriguez. Among staff, I especially liked Cloide Trujillo, whom I've mentioned, and Willie Jaramillo, the bursar. As time progressed—four years is a long time in the life of a young person—and some of our teachers and staff departed, my enthusiasm in the school diminished.

Three events occurred that I can tell briefly, the memory of which have remained with me. In the first instance, Ed Grant took us to meet Georgia O'Keeffe down the road in Abiquiú where she lived. Ed was imbued with a curiosity, and personal values, that I admired, and he had taken the time to cultivate a friendship with this grand lady of art. Georgia O'Keeffe's paintings are among my all time favorites in the world, no doubt because we got to know her at least a wee bit. She was interesting to me in the same way that her work on canvas is beautiful to everyone.

My second little story is a joke on me, but it is also to illustrate how loyalty and friendship can conquer all else as we bump into one another in life. One of my jobs at the high school was to supervise its cleaning, during my final year. As I entered this one classroom, desks were pushed up against the south wall, and Mr. Rodriguez, the principal, was bent over motioning to someone to "come out from under there." I laughed, as anyone would, and inquired, "What's the matter?" It turned out that Facundo Rodríguez had ordered Phillip, one of my schoolmates, to leave the room and board the school bus that would take him to religious instruction at the church. Phillip was refusing to comply. I wasn't too interested in the subject either, so I said to Mr. Rodriguez, "You can't do that. Remember the Dixon case? Kids in public school aren't required to attend church or any of that." Of course Facundo Rodriguez knew the Dixon case, it was a famous decision in New Mexico and the nation. But at our school for almost fifty years, kids were herded down to the Catholic church on Sunday, and no one objected, including me. Mr. Rodriguez simply said to me,

"Don't give me any trouble, go get on the bus." I quietly left and got on the bus. So did Phillip.

Well, I knew that Facundo Rodriguez, now deceased, cared for us more than almost anyone at the school. I would have done more than go to church for him.

Glenn George had been providing me with after-school assignments and materials to hone my math skills. In spring 1957, he entered me in a math competition that was sponsored by one of the universities, I presume with consent of the state department of education. Although I never learned my test score, as a result of the exam, New Mexico Tech provided me with a scholarship and a job that would help me to finance my entire four-year college career. Mr. George knew about my personal circumstance, and he wanted to make certain that I would have money enough to attend college.

▣

Members of the class of 1954 had some recollection of what was once the Spanish American Normal School. They occasionally seemed wistful that the Normal School had seen its better days. I merely assumed that was the way that upperclassmen were. Their other message to undergraduates seemed to be, hey, we're going to have fun this year and then we're moving on.

Boys' strongest interest continued to be athletics. A few teachers, Reuben Rose is the first to come in discussion, stood out for their popularity with students. In Mr. Rose's case, he attracted large numbers to his arts and crafts program. John Romero, the band director, was also popular with students and had strong participation from them. But the faculty had been depleted, by strife and quarrels with previous administration. This time the Children of the Normal School seemed to know the score, and they spoke about it.

English was becoming the prevailing language on the campus. The *Orquesta Típica* and Spanish and Mexican music were of the past. Popular music as interpreted by Frank Sinatra, Johnny Ray, the Andrews Sisters, the Four Lads, Nat Cole, and Patti Page were heard occasionally on radio. A couple of students interpreted the music of the time well: Sammy Esquibel, who sang Johnny Ray's songs, and Elva Jaramillo and Gloria Ortiz, who harmonized beautifully in the style that had become popular.

Older students had established a canteen, which dispensed candy and soft drinks. A ping-pong table occupied a good bit of space. I loved to play, although the older boys didn't seem interested in playing against this very small ninth grader.

There was music, but no dancing. In fact, I don't remember ever seeing girls at the canteen.

Rock and roll had not become the rage that would follow only two years later in the decade.

◩

I had brief acquaintance with upperclassmen during this first year; senior students don't usually have a lot to say to freshmen. But some of them did. Michael Branch, David Borunda, Jimmy Chávez, Sammy Esquibel, Richard García, Dennis Salazar, and Manny Torres were older boys, boisterous and cheerful. Sammy and Dennis were quieter, but I got to know them a little better by pestering them to play ping-pong with me; they would condescend to my obvious zeal, occasionally.

◩

Michael Branch was one of the younger members of the class of 1954.

Michael's mother was the former Anna McGrath from Roy, in northeastern New Mexico. His father, David Branch, also from Roy, had attended the Normal School in the 1920s.

Michael came to El Rito at the age of ten, in seventh grade, after his father perished in an automobile accident. As he became one of the Children of the Normal School, Michael joined with many of us who had needed a home and had come to El Rito, decade after decade. Although he had to learn to live with older kids, the nurturing care that he found in El Rito from teachers, staff, and students was most helpful. He remembered in our interview Lena and Wallace Archuleta, Reuben

Rose, Charles Solomon, Facundo Rodríguez, Tom Roybal, Louis Robert Trujillo, and many more friends.

Michael had good recollection of the fall of 1948, when typhoid fever broke out at the Normal School. Typhoid usually results when drinking water is contaminated. Mike guessed that he avoided the illness because he had built up immune resistance, acquired on the farm in Dilia, his previous home. Dilia is on the Pecos River, and in those days it was not uncommon that people drank water from the stream.

Mike worked for room and board, as did a majority of students. Supervision of boys was lax, which we welcomed. Aside from hazing by older students, life was pleasant and students felt "secure." The latter theme came up often in our discussions.

After high school, Michael attended the College of Santa Fé, and then served a hitch in the US Army.

Michael Branch resides in Santa Fé with his wife Maida. They have three sons. Michael is the owner of Branch Realty.

In January 2003, Michael Branch was appointed to the Board of Regents of Northern New Mexico Community College by Governor Bill Richardson. He continues to serve in this capacity of the school now known as Northern New Mexico College.

▣

David Borunda, also class of 1954, was born in Velarde in 1935.

David, his younger brother Archie, and their mother moved to Raton when the boys were very small. David had been partially orphaned after the death of his father.

David and Archie came to El Rito when David was in seventh grade; Archie was sixth. David lived in the Junior Building, dorm 1, and had no time for homesickness. Getting used to living with older children and making new friends were the order of the day, which took up most of his time.

David remembered that Archie was one of the children who contracted typhoid fever in 1948, and he had to go home. Archie returned to El Rito for ninth grade, after which he decided he did not want to stay at the Normal School any longer and he went home.

David enjoyed his studies and, after trying a couple of sports, he decided to stay with football, in which he took pride.

He remembered, as we spoke, the changes in campus environment after the departure of Joe Grant in 1951. Students, he remembered, found the period immediately following Grant's leaving more than a little unsettling.

David spoke often about his academic interests. For example, he remembered a paper he wrote in eighth grade, "Organization and Military Tactics of the Roman Army." History continued to be a favorite subject, and he singled out Frutoso López as a most helpful teacher.

Northern New Mexico Normal School provided a feeling of belonging and camaraderie, which David missed after graduating. David married and joined the Air Force in September 1954. He told me the experience in the US Air Force was a good one. He studied, learned Russian, and acquired the necessary clearance to work in the Intel Branch. He earned the rank of Staff Sergeant.

After a successful career in industry in eastern United States, he returned to New Mexico in the nineties. He renewed acquaintance with many of the alumni, took interest in the new institution, Northern New Mexico Community College, and was appointed to the board of its Foundation.

David and his wife Sheryl settled in Albuquerque. His children were David, Jr., Dennis, Donald, and Valerie. He had fourteen grandchildren and four great-grandchildren.

David had told me briefly about the death of his father, a soldier during World War II. Something that both he and I had noticed is that students at the Normal School seldom spoke about parents. After David understood my great interest in how New Mexico boys had fared during World War II, he explained to me: his father David left his mother Jenny and the boys, and enlisted in the US Army in Albuquerque in March 1941. Early in the war, he was wounded, came home to Alamogordo for a brief while, and returned to duty a year later in March 1942.

David's recollection was that his father was a cook during the war, and that he earned the Silver Star while in combat. Soon after David, Sr. arrived in Luzon, Philippine Islands, he was captured and taken to a prison camp, probably Cabanatuan. There were at least eight internment camps that the Japanese army had in the Philippines.

David spoke with a lot of emotion about what he had discovered about his dad; most of what he knew was from the newspaper and war records that he had sought. It is likely that David Borunda his father was moved to Camp O'Donnell. David learned that in June 1942, while his dad was trying to share food with a cousin Robert, a Japanese guard had killed his father.

David told me that students were eligible for a War Orphans' Scholarship, if their parent had died in a recent war. Edward Medina, then president of the school, David was pleased to note, recognized David as the orphaned child of this World War II soldier who had perished on Luzon.

David Borunda, class of 1954 died in spring 2011 in Albuquerque.

◙

Richard García, class of 1954 came to sixth grade at the Normal School in 1948.

The boarding school provided a "great atmosphere," is what Richard stated, although memory lingered that his parents had to come for him. He had become ill from typhoid infection and he "convalesced a long time," while in sixth grade.

After he returned, he liked the school, but he thought hazing was brutal. Richard echoed a concern spoken by other students: the school lacked in academic quality. *There were* teachers whom he appreciated, Reuben Rose being first among them.

During summers, he and Ted Martínez would return to Albquerque to work for the City and for Korber's Hardware Store, he remembered.

Richard played football with senior boys on the 1953 El Rito Eagles. As older boys, they influenced campus life beyond their involvement in sports, helping to shape opinion about teachers and their classes.

After high school, Richard attended the University of New Mexico for a year, then he enlisted in the US Navy. He remained in California after the Navy, attended Redlands University, and completed the BA degree. He then made a career in corporate real estate.

◻

Dennis Salazar, also class of 1954, was one of the boys who greeted me at El Rito; he was a dorm proctor.

Dennis arrived at the Normal School in 1947. His father was still living and operated a store in El Guache, but Dennis and brother Regino's mother had died. Although Dennis loved his new stepmother, he viewed El Rito "as God send" and described that a sense of belonging derived from the "feeling that students were brothers and sisters." Dennis remembered the typhoid epidemic of 1948 only vaguely. Neither he nor Regino became ill.

The job as dorm proctor in twelfth grade was a plum. He had had many jobs that were a great deal more difficult.

While he worked in the Junior Building, he had known Glenn George, a senior man who taught math, and Frank Byers, a coach.

Dennis was a serious young man and a good student. He tried baseball, basketball, and football at different times, but football was his sport. He was all-conference quarterback on a team that played single-wing, which meant that he was blocking back a good part of the time.

After high school, Dennis attended the University of New Mexico one year, after he took a job and married. He was soon drafted into the US Army.

He returned to Española from the Army and began to reintegrate into the community. He and Regino became successful in business, but remained dedicated to working with the community. Dennis was elected by voters to the 1969 Constitutional Convention of which Bruce King was chairman. Dennis got to know King well, and in 1971, when Bruce King became Governor, he appointed Dennis to the Board of Regents of the New Mexico Technical Vocational School at El Rito.

Dennis has maintained a long association with this institution since then. He became a founding board member of Northern New Mexico Community College and was appointed to the board again by Governor Bill Richardson in January 2003. In 2001, the Board of Regents, on my recommendation, named a building on the Española Campus that was used for general education as the Dennis Salazar Building.

◻

Priscilla Trujillo Schafer is also of the class of 1954.

Priscilla has an excellent memory and a recollection of times when she was a small child in El Rito in late 1930s and early 1940s. She grew up in Placitas in a house her parents built. The Trujillos were from El Rito and the Ortegas, her mother's family, from Vallecitos. Priscilla remembered that her father hauled freight from Denver, Colorado with the use of oxen. Readers may wish to recall that the present roadway to El Rito dates from about 1946.

Priscilla began school in the Placitas Elemenary School at age five; she spoke no English. Max Varoz, a great favorite among many former students, was principal of the school. Priscilla, a good student, was promoted from seventh to ninth grade, and so she was able to start high school early over at the Normal School. She was thirteen years old.

Priscilla recalled fondly that in 1948 her father owned a horse-drawn wagon when her brother Norberto graduated from the Normal School, first in his class—a merging of the old and modern times. Norberto soon thereafter departed to join the US Air Force. He subsequently returned to New Mexico State University to attend on the GI Bill. Priscilla told me these things with pride.

Priscilla loved the Normal School, but as in the case of many former students from El Rito, she has mixed feelings about how the school was run.

I met Priscilla when I was ninth grade; she was in twelfth, and very friendly and kind to me. Friendships that students made at the Normal School were many, and they have been surprisingly enduring.

She also spoke with fondness of teachers, Tom Roybal and Nina Myers, particularly. Ms. Myers counseled Priscilla to remain in school: she competed well academically and could overcome the indifference of administration toward day students.

Priscilla remained at the Normal School, but she recalled that parents had to petition the school to provide a room for lunch during those cold winter days in El Rito. She felt that some staff were unkind, and failed to provide transportation to students for after-school activities—ball games, band, and social events.

Priscilla Trujillo graduated from high school without many options since money was scarce, and there was then an absence of any financial aid for prospective students to attend college. Parents did not encourage daughters to continue studying. It was more common for girls to take a job.

In order to find work, however, Priscilla had to move to Santa Fé. She worked temporarily in the Department of Education, then housed at the old St. Michael's College. She renewed an acquaintance with Joseph Grant, who had become State Treasurer, and Priscilla went to work in that office. She enjoyed her years in the Treasurer's office, but in 1958 she decided to join the Missionary Sisters of Our Lady of Victory in Huntington, Indiana. She was in the Convent one year, but her failing health caused her to return to New Mexico.

Again in Santa Fé, Priscilla went to work in the State Engineer's office, then headed by Steve Reynolds. During this time she met James Schafer, whom she eventually married. The Schafers had children Dolores, Michael, and Patrick.

Priscilla Schafer was appointed to the Board of Regents of Northern New Mexico Community College by Governor Gary Johnson in January 1995. She and Jim had been living in El Rito where she was assisting in the care of her elderly father. This gave Priscilla opportunity to reacquaint herself with the old Normal School in its new incarnation. She grew to love the school, and told me that "The Community College was the best thing that could have happened here."

The Board of Regents on which Priscilla was serving rehired

me as president of the school in 1996; I had served in this capacity in the late 1980s. Priscilla was appointed to the Board of Regents for a second term, but she resigned to move back to Albuquerque. She has resided there since then.

Jim Schafer, Priscilla's husband and father to her three children, died in Albuquerque this past year.

□

Joe Martínez graduated with the class of 1954. I did not know Joe, in spite of having been in high school at El Rito during his last year there. He befriended me many years later when I was with Northern New Mexico Community College.

In fall 1953, I recall, students spoke with some excitement that Joe Martínez, a basketball star from the previous year who was not yet on campus, would be returning for his senior year. Someone invited me to the gymnasium, after Joe arrived, to watch him put on a one-man show——just him and the ball. He was a slender fellow, not too tall, perhaps five foot ten, but he was like a magician on the hardwood floor. He held the ball with unusually big hands, and he looked at it as though he were supplying it instructions on what it should do if it left his hands. Then he dazzled those watching by going through—"moves" they called them—gyrations that we wouldn't see in basketball until many years later from professional players like Julius Erving and, later, Kobe Bryant. Although this may seem an exaggeration, Joe Martínez was that good a ballplayer.

During the 1954 season, the El Rito Eagles, coached by Frank Byers, started slowly, but they won their last eight games prior to sweeping three more games in district tournament. Joe particularly shone against big men, usually from larger schools. The Eagles finished the season with 17 wins and eight losses, losing their final game on the way to the state tournament. The Eagles final loss was to Maxwell High School, which took second place at state. Maxwell had one player who measured 6'8", very tall in those days.

I heard Frank Byers say that this was the first time in their history that an Eagles' basketball team had won the district tournament.

Players on that squad included Joe Martínez, Sammy Esquibel, Lupe Juárez, Mike Jaramillo, Oscar Saiz, Eli Valdez, Estolano Márquez, Eligio Jaramillo, Dennis Branch, and Chris Delgado.

Joe Martínez died in winter 2005.

◻

Only a few students were conscious of the passing of an era. The class of 1955 included almost the last students of the Joe Grant period. I had gotten used to nostalgic tales of the time in which Grant was there, but even in 1955 the frequency of these stories diminished.

Add to this that teachers were leaving: Corine Myers and Sam Ortega after spring 1954. Reuben Rose, Ed Grant, Humbero Gurulé, and Frank Byers all departed after the 1954–1955 school year. Older notions of tradition, things that mattered and those that didn't, were leaving or gone with the loss of institutional memory.

Members of the class of 1955 seemed a bit more accessible to a kid like me in tenth grade, and I got to know some of them. They were bright. I remember their remarks about the school for their accuracy and cogency.

◻

Esperanza Baca was one of the students who graduated in 1955.

She has a sister Socorro, who was in my ninth grade class, but Socorro elected to graduate a year early, in 1956.

Esperanza first attended a one-room school in El Rito. In second grade, she enrolled at the Normal School.

Esperanza was a very good student, and she was valedictorian of the class of 1955. A very good friend of hers, Arlene Gonzales, was salutatorian. I found them inseparable when we were in school.

Esperanza told me that she wished that she had learned to write well in high school, and she thought that the school should have taught more about New Mexico history and geography. Esperanza, always serious about scholarship, did not feel that there was a great deal to be learned at the Normal School.

One of the students whom I got to know well in our adult life, Esperanza explained to me that she had come from a family of very modest means. School was important, but she had to work. Summers she would work at Gene Autry Studios in Santa Fé. Immediately upon graduation from high school, she enrolled at New Mexico Highlands University, on a music scholarship. The scholarship did not provide for all expenses, so she had to do janitorial work at the University.

After she had been at Highlands a semester, Esperanza met Nelson Gonzales, her future husband. Esperanza and Nelson, from Taos, soon left Las Vegas and Highlands for Los Angeles where she enrolled at California State University. In time, back in New Mexico, Esperanza reenrolled at Highlands and earned a master's degree.

Esperanza and Nelson have devoted careers to public education. She was principal of the El Rito Elementary School, a position for which she gained the respect of the community and area educators. Nelson was counselor at the New Mexico Technical Vocational School at one time, but he is best remembered as superintendent of the Mesa Vista School District.

Esperanza and Nelson are both retired, and reside in El Rito. She has been writing a history of El Rito and its immediate area. She has shared freely in her historical knowledge with me for this book.

▣

Albert Esparcen is from Trujillo, which is forty miles southeast of Las Vegas where he would have had to travel to high school had he not learned about the Normal School from one of his teachers.

Albert graduated with the class of 1955. He attended elementary school through eighth grade at the Ventanas Consolidated Schools. While in seventh and eighth grades he encountered a teacher who was familiar with Northern New Mexico Normal School, Horacio Ulibarrí. He spoke with Albert and his parents about the Normal School, and the parents resolved to help Albert go there. It helped that another student from Trujillo, Salomon Archuleta, was at El Rito.

Although Albert's mother spoke English, the family spoke Spanish at home, and so Albert's first language became Spanish. Albert described life in Trujillo in those days as "socially impoverished," since there wasn't much contact culturally outside of the community. There were no electricity or water systems. The family had a battery-operated radio that provided entertainment, mostly country-western and Mexican music. Water was taken from a cistern, which also served to refrigerate food. He commented that they tended to be quite self-sufficient in living like pioneers.

Albert's mother accompanied him to El Rito on his first trip. They took a bus in Trujillo to Española, then the mail truck from there to El Rito. Albert tended to stay on campus weekends and holidays, where he worked part time. Albert stated about the Normal School, "I loved it from day one."

Albert was a popular boy. He played football and was on the boxing team. He was also on the track team, as I recall. He was one of several serious students, but he found time to court his girl friend, Carol Medina, from Abiquiú, whom he would marry after high school.

Albert's memories of the Normal School are pleasant. Although there was some hazing, he felt the idea was to endure it and "fit in." He appreciated that there was little supervision of the boys, although traveling off campus was not easy. Students would hitch hike to Española, not knowing whether there would be a ride available to the campus at the end of the day.

Albert's education was "adequate." Chuck Solomon, who taught English, stood out as the teacher who was of greatest help.

Albert enlisted in the US Air Force after high school and married Carol. He returned to Santa Fé to attend college. He loved the College of Santa Fé and graduated *cum laude*, with honors. He subsequently completed a doctoral program in public health and physical rehabilitation at the University of New Mexico.

He "tracked down" Horacio Ulibarrí in 1985 to thank him for his personal interest and support about thirty years back in Trujillo.

Albert had a long and beneficial career with the US Public Health Services, from which he is retired.

Albert and Carol and their family have resided in Santa Fé.

◙

Lupe Juárez, also class of 1955, lived almost half of his childhood in El Rito.

Lupe is one of the Children of the Normal School who arrived at the Normal School early in their lives, for fifth grade in 1947.

Lupe and Benito, an older brother, were from Albuquerque. Lupe had lived with grandparents and with his mother, Chonita Juárez, while he attended East San José Elementary School. His mother knew a boy who had attended El Rito, felt encouraged by reports, and sent Lupe's brother Benito there first.

When Lupe arrived at the boarding school as a boy, he felt harassed initially, but soon found himself happy and secure, especially happy about receiving three square meals per day.

Lupe Juárez in fall 1953 demonstrated his athleticism on the football field. He wasn't a big kid, perhaps average for high school in those days. But once on the ball field or ball court, his ability, in all sports, immediately rose above everyone as though driven by spirit. Not only was he the best player present, but he seemed also the smartest player.

I asked him which was his favorite sport. His reply was, "Whichever sport was in season."

That fall, as an end on the football team, he put on a demonstration of his deceptiveness as a pass receiver and a pass-catching ability that everyone who saw him spoke about. He was named as a First Team All-American by Parade Magazine, which would pick the top players in the nation yearly. Lupe was the only All-American in the history of the high school at El Rito.

In baseball, Lupe could pitch, play shortstop, and hit the ball. I want to emphasize: he knew the game and he played with uncanny intelligence. He knew what to do in a manner that seemed instinctive, but smart.

He was on a strong basketball team of 1954 that won the district. It was one of the Normal School's better teams.

The greatest demonstration of leadership that I have seen on a basketball court was exhibited by Lupe Juárez in a game against Pojoaque in the winter of 1955. We always knew Lupe was a "money player." This is the guy you go to when you have to have that final shot to win a game. But this particular Saturday afternoon Lupe astounded the few thousand people in attendance at a game in which Pojoaque led the El Rito Eagles by 13 points with three minutes to go in the ballgame. Lupe would receive the ball in-bounds and dribble across court to the top of key, go up in the air, hang a second or two, and fire two points. He must have repeated this eight or ten times, because surely Pojoaque's Elks scored at least once or twice. But each time the Eagles got the ball, they would give it to Lupe, who would fire it cleanly through the basket from the same spot at the top of the key. El Rito won this semifinal tournament game against a good team. I have not seen another such demonstration of take-charge basketball.

Lupe was also a performer, always conscious of his audience. He moved with the grace of an artist or dancer and the sublimity of dry ice. In short, he dazzled those watching him play.

A kid with this leadership ability should have been helped to develop further. He was not. In northern New Mexico, athletes like Lupe were not taken aside and developed beyond the ability with which they were born.

In the early sixties, I had the pleasure of working with Lupe Juárez at ACF Industries, a contractor for the Atomic Energy Commission, on the south side of Albuquerque.

Lupe resides in Albuquerque, his hometown.

回

Ted Martínez was a member of the class of 1955.

Ted, an Albuquerque boy from the old Martíneztown, went to El Rito in sixth grade. He was from a large family, and he welcomed the privacy and attention that he found at the the Normal School.

Ted was one of the children who were hit hardest by the spread of typhoid fever on campus in 1948. He lived with the illness on campus for about a month and a half, then he convalesced in quarantine at home until April of the following year, 1949, when he was finally released by the Health Department. He did not return to El Rito until tenth grade, a long time to be gone in the life of a boy.

I first saw Ted in the evening of my first day at El Rito, a Sunday. I walked into Cutting Hall, a clean, well-lit small auditorium with a stage for performances, and a hardwood floor. This evening there was a movie and what I thought would be an opportunity to greet students. Instead, there were isles of seats, with a wide space down the middle separating genders: girls on the right, boys on the left.

The buzzing sound of about eighty or more voices stopped, and I saw a slender young man, his suntan accenting the light-color shirt he wore, off toward the side in deep discussion with a senior woman, obviously the girls' dorm matron, as she was called. After a few hand and arm gestures and nods all around—another matron had joined the discussion—there was a complete hush. The announcement was made that boys and girls could sit where they wished and socialize for the evening...a wide cheer and applause from the students.

My first thought was now there is a master of politics, a diplomat. This boy will go far, this dark kid in the light, loose shirt.

The boy was Ted Martínez, of course, and for reasons unknown to me, he decided as time went on to be my friend. He would later tell people that I had helped tutor him in math; I don't remember that. In fact, my only memory of these small study groups was about girls, understandably.

Ted was a serious student and an equally committed athlete. He worked at running well, and he was the fastest man at the school. He did exceptionally well in 100 and 220 yard dash, but it was in football that he merits telling another story.

In fall of 1954, the football Eagles were preparing for an important game against Aztec High School. The Eagles had a good, although small team. El Rito had won its district championship in the previous year, but had lost to the Aztec Tigers in a bi-district regional playoff. The Eagles were fun to watch, this being the team that included Lupe Juárez and Ted Martínez, with a solid group of senior boys. I knew, however, that they were no match for the Aztec Tigers, whom they would play a second time in less than a year.

A small group of us got the idea that I should do a play-by-play of the game on a portable tape recorder, in case one of the Santa Fé radio stations might be interested in replaying it. We hurriedly set it up; it worked just fine.

On a bright, sunny afternoon the teams squared off. El Rito won the toss, Aztec would kick off to our boys. As the teams lined up, the Eagles looked like junior high kids up against a group of tall Aztec farm boys. Aztec kicked off, I can't remember who received for El Rito, it didn't matter. I had turned on the tape recorder and begun to describe the teams on the field, and the tense expectation of the fans on hand for the game, mostly students.

As soon as the ball was caught, the Eagles huddled around the ball to the surprise of all of us watching, and to the befuddlement of the Aztec Tigers. Each of the Eagles came out of the huddle crouched as though hiding the football, running toward their goal beyond the boys from Aztec. The Tigers tried to figure out who had the ball. Down the left sideline, completely undetected and all alone, went our fastest running back, Ted Martínez, headed for paydirt. There wasn't a Tiger near him. My friends and accomplices would later say that I had screamed into the microphone, "He's headed downfield, look at that son-of-a-gun go!" but in stronger language, of course.

The game ended with a score of 20 to 6, Aztec. The ruse had worked, and we enjoyed our moment after Ted's touchdown.

Incident after incident of fun is told about our days at El Rito. This is one I like.

Ted passed up the second half of his senior year at El Rito, and enrolled at the University of New Mexico. We have spoken often about the quality of education that we received at Northern New Mexico Normal School, Ted believes it was sufficient to prepare him for college. He had to take no preparatory courses at the University.

Ted joined the US Marine Reserve during college, but he was drafted just the same. He enrolled in officer candidate school, and received a military commission. He retired from the Marine Reserve later on as a captain.

Ted began a career in Albuquerque in earnest after having received a master's degree at the University. He taught for a few years at Río Grande High School, and subsequently entered the employment of the University of New Mexico. He recalled, as we spoke, how much he enjoyed working at UNM, where he served a couple of important assignments with Dr. Ferrel Heady, president of UNM at the time. Ted first ran the Student Union, but in a few years he became assistant to the president, probably owing to his negotiating skills. This was the period of the late sixties and early seventies in which student unrest reached a crescendo at the University. These were tense times in higher education in the Nation. Arguments centered around civil rights, with Hispanic students intent an asserting their own rights, resulting in an interesting period. Ted handled his responsibilities well.

Almost simultaneously, Ted ran for a position on the Albuquerque Public School Board, and won. He held the position for several years during Albuquerque's explosive growth in student population. Ted worked with Superintendents Ernest Stapleton and Frank Sanchez, whom he admired.

In 1984, Ted was appointed executive secretary of the Board of Educational Finance by Governor Toney Anaya. Ted called me on the phone as though we had broken off a conversation from just yesterday, when, in fact, I hadn't seen him in many years. He invited me to come to the BEF to work; I agreed to it. This occurred about the same time that Governor Anaya named a group of us to study the matter of how to help the universities to become stronger and more effective. Fred Harris, professor at the University of New Mexico and an experienced political figure, was our chairman. Our efforts gave rise to the Commission on Higher Education. After establishment of the Commission, Ted continued as director of the new organization until 1989.

Ted Martínez was appointed president of the Albuquerque Technical-Vocational Institute in July 1989, in which capacity he served for five years until his retirement.

Ted resides in Albuquerque with his wife Dolores. They have daughters Demetria and Elena, and son Dominic. They also have three grandchildren.

◻

Few things are more difficult for a high school kid than the departure of someone you liked, or admired, or loved, or all of these plus other emotions.

During these interviews and discussions with former students of the early fifties, inevitably the name of our teachers come up, most frequently that of Reuben Rose. I didn't know Reuben at the Normal School, not very well, anyway. But the response of students with whom I have spoken about Reuben Rose is extraordinary.

Reuben came to the Normal School in the fall of 1952, from Highlands University where he had newly graduated. He, and several of his classmates, took jobs in northern New Mexico that fall of 1952, and an impressive group they were. Reuben and Chuck Solomon came to the Normal School; our friends John Aragón and Willie Sánchez settled in Española for a brief period.

Reuben was an artist, more interested in crafts. He was also a jazz enthusiast. Children of the Normal School tended to flock to his classes, both to learn crafts and to pick up on music and culture.

For his part, Reuben seemed to understand our kids, perhaps owing to his own background. He had been born in Poland in 1920 to parents whose name was Resnik. They first came to Windsor, Canada, then to the United States. This need to acculturate, to become American, to share in the American culture and its dream, were perhaps what Reuben and our kids in northern New Mexico had in common.

Reuben had a kindred spirit and colleague at El Rito, Chuck Solomon, briefly. I met and got to know Reuben and Chuck in our adult lives, and I liked and admired both of them.

For the purpose of this book, I asked Betty Rose, Reuben's wife, to interview with me. She provided more about his background, which gave me a greater appreciation for this tolerant, understanding man whom I had spent many hours with in Santa Fé simply getting to know.

Betty and Reuben had met in Brooklyn, New York, and they had married nine month later in July 1947. Reuben was a veteran of World War II, and they had met on his return to New York City.

Betty enjoyed living at El Rito, and the students who visited with them frequently. She had a job as a social worker in this north central region, but she found time to entertain. And to have children. Reuben and Betty's oldest son Larry was born while the Roses were in El Rito.

Betty hated it when Reuben quit teaching. He left the Normal School in summer 1954.

Reuben passed away a few years ago. Betty lives in Santa Fé in the same house in which I visited with the Roses, usually on Reuben's birthday.

▣

Nineteen fifty-five brought a change in culture in the United States that went unrecognized by only a few people. This was the advent of rock and roll. I liked it, and signs were that most of the kids at the Normal School did, too.

About the same time, I had joined kids from Albuquerque and Santa Fé who listened to radio late at night. We could pick up a strong station from Shreveport, Louisiana that played blues all night long. African American musicians were masters of the blues, as they were in jazz, and a new invention, rhythm and blues. We knew about these things, mostly from radio.

White America, kids mostly, studied this music and came up with another version out of the South, which they called Rockabilly. But the guy who made a splash in 1955 was Bill Haley, with a song I found barely interesting, "Rock Around the Clock." It sold lots of records, and helped with the explosion of this big beat, rock and roll.

We liked all of the new artists: Chuck Berry, Little Richard, Fats Domino, and several more, and, of course, the king himself, Elvis Presley. There were many others, often copies of African American artists and their music, but Elvis was genuine.

▣

Estolano Márquez, class of 1956, was a pleasant, soft-spoken young man from San Ysidro.

Estolano was courting Olivia Salazar, a student from Velarde. One of her brothers had been my friend back at the elementary school. Estolano and Olivia were exceptionally friendly; still are.

Estolano was preceded at the Normal School by his sister Cassie Márquez, class of 1949.

For many of the boys at the school, in particular those from rural villages far from a high school, El Rito was a haven for sports, football and basketball, especially. Estolano was just interested in playing ball, not in the attention that normally came with it. He was a good runner, swift as opposed to just fast, and a good trackman who loved team sports, also.

During Estolano's senior year at the Normal School, an interesting change was taking place, unexpectedly. After the spring of 1955, Frank Byers had resigned as teacher and coach of the basketball Eagles. His teams had been quite successful. Most of us expected a letdown. The school seemed to have little recruiting ability, it was still fairly isolated, it didn't pay its employees very well, and not a lot had changed in this regard. The Normal School hired Vince Martínez, the football coach, to fill the vacancy left with Byers's departure. Expectations for the basketball program were not high.

Estolano played on a team that spring of 1956 in which he was the only senior, the older boy. He knew his coach well; Estolano had played football for "Marty," as Vince Martínez was known.

The Eagles started the season showing some promise. A team that included Estolano, Dennis Branch, Ralph Martínez, David Valdez, and Porfirio Sánchez, a senior, a junior, and three sophomores seemed strong. Dennis Branch started the year showing signs of the prolific scorer that he would become. It was an interesting team that kept getting better and better.

I called Estolano on the telephone, because I knew that he would have insights concerning the success of this team, and Marty's teams in subsequent years. In 1956, the Eagles posted a record of 17 wins and five losses in the regular season, they won the district by beating a good Pojoaque team 51 to 47 in the final game, and they finished third in the state tournament. This had been El Rito's most successful basketball season ever. It was a preview of the next few years in basketball at El Rito.

Estolano explained to me what had happened. This was a team of strong kids, quick and fast, but what mattered most was the superb conditioning of Vince Martínez's teams. Estolano knew, he said to me, that the best was yet to come as the young group of players matured.

Estolano finished high school, married Olivia, and moved briefly to his home in San Ysidro. Jobs were in Albuquerque, where they subsequently moved.

Estolano and Olivia have resided in Albuquerque with their family.

▣

Robert Torres, the third of four brothers to attend the Normal School, also graduated in 1956.

Bob's family was from Black Lake, deep in the Sangre de Cristo range of mountains, where winter snowfalls help produce the lush green grass of summer. The Torres family were ranchers; they raised cattle.

Indalesio was the first of the brothers to attend the Normal School; he graduated in 1950. I met him briefly during the alumni reunion of 1998.

"Manny" followed at the school; he graduated in 1954. Manuel, always affable and good natured, worked abroad for many years. I saw him only occasionally. He is deceased.

Luis, the youngest brother, I have written about in these page with his class of 1959.

Bob Torres knew that he had to leave Black Lake in order to attend high school. Education was very important in his family, and he should attend high school, at least. Taos, the nearest town, was not an option. Manny was at El Rito, a good reason to go there, which is what Bob did in fall 1953.

Bob loved the campus, although he realizes today that it was never to seem as beautiful and orderly as it did on his arrival. He enjoyed dormitory life, too, and seldom felt like just going home.

Not homesick, Bob adjusted well to other students, knew whom to befriend. He knew boarding schools could be special, and this one was.

He was pleased with the education that he received at the Normal School. He referred to Reuben Rose, as we spoke, as an icon of the school. Rose was a favorite of so many students. Bob was later a better student, in college, but the Normal School provided a valuable lesson: how to get along with people.

Bob said that the "outside world" was of little importance at the time. "We were very secure. Ike was president. Life was so good at El Rito that we really didn't need the world." Bob explained that it was not as though students lived there in isolation. Bob grew to love the music of the 1950s and he read. He remembered Somerset Maughm— and his novel *Of Human Bondage* that he got from Ed Grant—and a biography of Mahatma Ghandi, who impressed Bob with his humility. Television was not important at the time, although the quality of things he saw was excellent, even if quantity was not overwhelming.

Bob enjoys reminiscing about old times at the Normal School. Joking was always a good device to allay hostility, and Bob mastered it. He managed to maintain contact with old friends through the organization of alumni.

Bob became a quiet, studious man. He has an architectural degree from California Polytechnical State University in San Luis Obispo, CA; he also has a law degree. He has traveled, having worked in Saudi Arabia for several years. He is worldly in ways that few Americans tend to be. He has told me in conversation about his love for London, England and its theaters.

Bob Torres resides in Taos.

◙

George Luján was on track to graduate with the class of 1956. But in August 1954, a month before his junior year, George enlisted in the US Navy.

George is like many of the Children of the Normal School whom I've known. He had to overcome adversity in order to succeed in life, and to plan his life usually with only his own counsel. He did it well.

George told me about himself in an interview at the community college in Española.

He enrolled at El Rito in 1949 in seventh grade. He had been born in 1937, and orphaned at the age of five in Santa Fé when both his parents died one year apart. George had two brothers and a sister, but he lived with an uncle for a while. A bit later he moved in with his mother's mom; she cared for him. George's brothers lived in the house and paid grandma ten bucks a month. After a while, George's brothers rented their own home, and George lived with them.

George said he "roamed the streets of Santa Fé," although a small boy. He talked about these matters with amusement, not wonderment, or regret, only a wry smile. Adventures that were available were fun: in the vicinity not far was the New Mexico State Penitentiary where George would walk by and make friends with inmates who would be working at maintaining the grounds of the institution.

George and his brothers lived on West Manhattan; it was a friendly neighborhood. He attended St. Francis Elementary School. George learned how to earn a nickel, as a young boy, by retailing *piñón*, pine nuts, in his walks around Santa Fé.

George's brother Raymond encouraged him to stay in school, which he did, and eventually George made his way to the Normal School.

George loved the campus. He speaks highly of the care that students showed toward one another. "You either liked El Rito and got along (with other students) or you didn't," he told me. Dennis Salazar and Charlie Aragón were a couple of older boys who were helpful to George. George remembered fondly his typing teacher, Viola Ulibarrí.

After eleventh grade, George left the Normal School to join the Navy. He studied and earned the General Equivalency Diploma (GED) for which the state of New Mexico awarded him the diploma. In 1948, George enrolled at the University of New Mexico, where he met a former schoolmate, Louise Archuleta from Truchas. George and Louise married soon thereafter.

Years later, in 1973, George came to El Rito once again, this time to work at the New Mexico Technical Vocational School. The school provided him housing on campus, and he took his meals in the cafeteria.

George returned to California in order to enroll at the University of California at Irvine, in 1978. George remarried after spending a few years on his own.

I saw George for the first time after high school in 1979, when he was purchasing agent at Northern New Mexico Community College. George worked there until retirement.

George and his wife Kathy live in Española.

◙

Several youngsters attended the Normal School, but were unable to stay until they graduated from the high school. Circumstance, often the need to earn a living, required some of our schoolmates to leave the school. There were many more Children of the Normal School who, like George Luján, left the school, but have managed to maintain contact with us.

A few names come immediately to mind: Richard Chávez from Albuquerque; Laura Padilla, Las Vegas; Lorraine Maestas, Española; Amarante "Shadow" Sánchez, Albuquerque; and Lee Leyba from Santa Fé. I mention these names because they have remained active with the association of alumni and supported this singularly important effort that has made it possible for Children of the Normal Schools to remain in contact with one another.

◙

Amarante Sánchez was another Albuquerque boy whom I met in the fall of 1953. I don't know the origin of "Shadow," whom people recognize more readily than his given name. I remember him for his bright, energetic, and pleasant personality.

Amarante was preceded at the Normal School by his brothers, Melecio, Leo, and Ray Sanchez. The brothers were student athletes, remembered long after their graduation and departure from the

Normal School. In a school in which the students delighted in providing nicknames, the brothers were known as the *Gololsos*, and each in turn in the singular, probably having to do with nothing but that the name occurred to someone.

Amarante became a successful businessman, after a stint in the armed services and travel. He is a strong supporter of the Alumni Association, an independent organization. He made special effort to convey to me that students of Northern New Mexico Normal School were his family.

◙

My classmates were the class of 1957

In summer 2007, a few of us planned a brief reunion, in Albuquerque, since the majority of former students no longer resided in northern New Mexico. Twelve of our members were able to attend: Polly Abeyta, Cecilia Archuleta, Lydia Archuleta, Tillie Esquibel, Leo García, Olivia Gómez, Lee Leyba, Lorraine Maestas, Gerald Martínez, Ida Montoya, Laura Padilla, and Sigfredo Maestas. Our guests included Celerino Archuleta, Beatrice Martínez, Florence Coriz, Albert Esparcen, Carol Medina, and Ted Martínez. Spouses of our former schoolmates were present, also.

Some of our classmates were ill, or could not attend for other reasons. We learned that fully twelve of our classmates had been then deceased.

◙

One of our classmates, whom some of us remembered fondly, was Nancy Zamora. Nancy was a girl from Trampas, when she came to the Normal School. She and her husband Joe Montoya, from Las Vegas, were supporters of the organization of alumni.

After Nancy's passing, Joe visited the campus several times in remembrance.

◙

The class of 1957 may be remembered for having abolished

student hazing, which most dictionaries aptly define as requirement to do work, often humiliating, for someone on penalty of punishment for disobeying an order. The practice again raised its awful head in later years, but the class of 1957 eschewed such nonsense.

My fondest recollection was with regard to the large number of very bright kids in a relatively small class of students: Cecilia Archuleta, Lydia Archuleta, Tillie Esquibel, Lugie Rosanne Martínez, Connie Valdez and Nancy Zamora. Sigfredo Maestas was class valedictorian; Leo García was salutatorian.

◻

Lee Leyba was a boy from Santa Fé who came to the Normal School for ninth grade in 1953.

I recently asked Lee for this interview because, although he didn't stay for twelfth grade at El Rito, he cherishes the memory of the Normal School and he has supported the Alumni Association for several years.

Lee was a cheerful and fun-loving boy. Many years later, as he spoke to me he echoed my sentiments and those of other schoolmates, in expressing his love of the Normal School as home. His depth of feeling is greater than one hears from most students, although they speak in a similar vein.

Lee attended the Guadalupe Elementary School as a small boy, and following that he enrolled at Harrington Junior High School. His experiences in those schools were not totally satisfactory, from his standpoint. He would discover later at El Rito that what his previous schools had lacked was the ability to make him feel wanted, and that he was worth an investment in time and effort. In short, the attention that he received lacked a personal quality.

At El Rito, Lee felt very much at home. The teachers liked him, as did the principal of the high school, Facundo Rodriguez. Kids liked Lee, and any disagreements quickly dissipated among a barrage of humor, easy banter.

Lee left school after eleventh grade and joined the US Navy, in order to begin to earn a living. He married and he and his small family lived in California.

After the Navy, Lee joined the US Coast Guard where he made a career. The Coast Guard offered opportunities for Lee to further his education, and he received training in the type of intelligence work that is stressed in that branch of the Nation's military defense.

In Albuquerque, Lee was active with the League of United Latin American Citizens (LULAC).

Lee enjoys travel, particularly in southern Europe. He and his wife Dolly reside in Albuquerque.

回

We had learned to expect a strong basketball team in 1956–1957. The football season was a successful one, but there was anticipation about the approach of winter and the new basketball season. The Eagles disappointed no one.

Marty molded a group that was still young, Dennis Branch, David Valdez, Ralph Martínez, Randy Velarde, and Porfirio Sánchez, into a powerful starting five. He added Sam Martínez, John Jaramillo, Chris Quintana, Albert Sánchez, and Joseph Valdez, very young boys, to provide even greater strength to the 1957 El Rito Eagles.

The season started and the Eagles reeled off seven straight wins before losing a game, over at West Las Vegas, in an off-night. They then went on another tear for eight games, before losing to Los Alamos, a larger, class A, school. Along the way, the Eagles breezed through to the finals of the Río Grande conference tournament, before losing to Española, 64 to 62.

The Eagles didn't lose another game. They roared through district and regional tournaments to gain their place at the state tournament. Because the Eagles didn't play an easy regular season schedule, even the state tournament seemed a breeze. The El Rito Eagles culminated their most successful season in the school's thirty-five year history by beating a fairly big and sound team from Ruidoso by a score of 88 to 44.

回

Most of the buzz during the state tournament was about Dennis

Branch, who had averaged close to thirty points per game and scored 43 points in a semifinal game in the tournament. Forty-three points set a record for the state tournament, but it was to be broken the following night by a boy named Kim Nash from Hobbs, who scored 45. Dennis, the more consistent player, was named all-state along with almost the entire starting unit for El Rito.

Dennis Branch, a boy from Coyote, was a towering figure in New Mexico high school basketball in 1956 and 1957. The statement is metaphorical, of course. He played center on teams, although he was about five feet eleven inches tall. He played a single post because of an excellent jumping ability. He had a great feign to the basket and he could fake the opposition out of its shoes. In two successive seasons he averaged about 28 and 30 points per game. His total point production is still unsurpassed, I believe.

◫

Vincent Martínez brought pride to the boys who played on his teams, and joy to those of us watching them. The Eagles played good, fast basketball, strong defense, and an occasional full court press to baffle the opposition. It was a high-scoring team, in addition.

Marty was a quiet and humble man. In April 2010, former players and students, I among them, attended a luncheon in Los Lunas in tribute to the deeds of this good man.

◫

The last semester of the class of 1957 is now but a dream that fleeted past us. The anticipation of leaving, and preparing to go to a new campus—I would go to New Mexico Tech almost immediately on graduating high school—made me lose consciousness of my immediate situation.

For example, I was only vaguely aware that the school was having difficulty acquiring funds from the state for the many repairs that the campus needed. I was aware of the disrepair of the campus, but knew little about the school's lack of money. I didn't know then that the Normal School's funding agency, the Board of Educational Finance, had, in fact, reduced the school's budget and requested that it dip into its small fund balance to support its operation.

This was but the beginning of a period, lasting almost ten years, in which the Normal School would have difficulty obtaining much support, from the legislature and Governor, for its high school program.

The class of 1958 marked another change, probably more visible to those of us who had attended school during the middle part of the decade. There were fewer students from cities: Albuquerque and Santa Fé, in particular.

◻

David Trujillo graduated with the class of 1958.

David was a boy from El Rito, whose brothers and sisters also attended the Normal School. I have written about their mother Cloide earlier in these pages.

David began at Placitas Elementary School. Cleo Martínez taught first grade, and Margaret Martínez taught second. David moved to the Normal School for fourth grade. During high school, David stated, he had very little connection with the school, with the exception that he played in the band, in which he exceled. David is a trumpeter, and he credited John Romero for stimulating his interest in music.

David's comments about the treatment accorded to day students by the school echo the sentiments of schoolmates whose views I have tried to represent in this book.

I learned from David that in his early years at the Normal School, the music program was augmented by the *Orquesta Típica*, sponsored by John Villa. David remembered John and his wife Dora.

David Trujillo attended New Mexico Highlands University, where he continued studying music after his graduation at the Normal School. He became a music teacher.

David married Priscilla Ceballes from Española. David and Priscilla made their home in Santa Fé until Priscilla was hired by the New Mexico Technical Vocational School in July 1977 when the family moved to Española.

David directed the music program at Santa Fé Indian School, prior to his retirement. David and Priscilla, surrounded by children and grandchildren, live in Española.

◻

Robert Archuleta, a boy from Cuba, was of the class of 1958.

Robert's mother, a schoolteacher, wanted Robert to have a better education than was available in Cuba. He attended schools at Allison James in Santa Fé and Menaul High School in Albuquerque, prior to enrolling at El Rito. The Normal School had been known to kids in Cuba, and a few students, some related to Robert, had attended the school.

Robert was a talented musician, and he played guitar in the 1950s, mostly rock and roll. He also played on the school's football team as a running back.

Robert attended New Mexico Tech and New Mexico State University, receiving a bachelor of science degree at the latter institution. Following his university studies, he worked for the federal government in administering public lands used for animal grazing.

Robert, an avid fisherman, and his wife Jean live in southern Colorado on the banks of the Conejos River.

◻

Lucas Trujillo was also class of 1958.

Lucas, a boy from El Rito, followed Norberto and Priscilla at the Normal School. The two are his brother and sister.

Lucas started school in Placitas when Max Varoz was principal there.

Lucas, an unassuming individual, was a good student throughout high school. He played football three years, as a running back. Lucas's favorite teacher, as he thought during our interview, was Tom Roybal who taught Spanish.

During Lucas's senior year, the Eagles won their district in football, and they faced the Aztec Tigers, again, in a regional playoff. Lucas recalled traveling to Aztec and "playing under the lights" against a very strong Aztec Tiger squad, who advanced to the state final game of 1958.

Lucas returned to El Rito after college and taught math at the Normal School from 1964 to 1969. During his first year, C.H. Robinson was superintendent and Melvin Cordova was principal of the high school. Lucas later assisted Vince Martinez with the athletic program.

Lucas and other teachers suspected that the high school was to be phased out. The state dictated that the high school be discontinued, but teachers were not informed of the action until the 1968–1969 school year. His recollection was that, "We all voted for the bond issue," that authorized creation of the Mesa Vista School District.

After the high school closed at the Normal School, Lucas took a job at the new Mesa Vista High School in Ojo Caliente. He taught there until he retired in 1994, 25 years later.

Lucas Trujillo has helped in developing the new water system for El Rito and Northern New Mexico College. He is on the present board of directors of the organization, the El Rito Water Users' Association.

Lucas and his family reside in El Rito.

◻

In 1958, Juan García left the Normal School not to return until years later. His parents felt that the Normal School was short of teachers and so they sent Juan to school at The Abbey in Canyon City, Colorado. The Colorado school, under the auspices of Benedictine priests, had a strong academic program. After high school, Juan enrolled at the College of Santa Fé for the BA degree.

In 1965, Juan joined the staff at El Rito and remained when it became the New Mexico Technical Vocational School, and then Northern New Mexico Community College. During his first years at the school, Juan worked in student financial aid and in the Learning Center.

For years afterward, Juan García directed the High School Equivalency Program, which he brought to the campus. Juan retired in this capacity with Northern New Mexico Community College.

Juan has continued to assist Northern New Mexico College by incorporating it into the El Rito Water Users, an organization that we helped found when I was president of the community college. Juan told me that a very adequate well has been supplying water to its users, a welcome change in this small basin in which good water has always been scarce.

◻

Students at the Normal School continued doing what they had always done, unimpeded by winds that might have disturbed them had they known about changes that they would portend.

◻

In 1958, the state champion Eagles prepared for another basketball season, not as spectacularly successful as the previous year, but a solid showing nevertheless.

Ralph Martínez, David Valdez, and Randy Velarde formed the nucleus from the previous year of another strong team. During the regular season, including an invitational tournament, the Eagles won 20 games and lost six. They won the district championship again by avenging two regular season losses to Pojoaque and beating the Elks in the final game. This very good Eagles team was eliminated from further competition in bi-district regional play.

◻

The Normal School had undergone another name change, not of its own choosing. Since about 1956, the legal name of the school was Northern New Mexico State School, a name no one seemed to like. This reflected, possibly, the fact that the New Mexico legislature and governors were getting weary of supporting a high school at El Rito. The Board of Regents defended the school and its mission in the best manner it could. But it, too, could do nothing more than prepare the school for change, and, in the best manner possible, guard its integrity.

In insisting that throughout this narrative we are discussing the same school historically, I continue to refer to it as the Normal School as does its constitutional mandate.

�«

After the 1957–1958 school year, the Board of Regents announced its intention to reinitiate a junior college on the campus. Although signals from Santa Fe about the type of program that the state would support at the Normal School were mixed, depending on who was in state office issuing the message, the Board of Regents seemed to have the support of the executive director of the Board of Educational Finance, in this instance. The Board received the message not to reinitiate vocational education, so the junior college was a logical choice.

The Board of Regents did not renew the employment contract with Clory B. Tafoya, whose three-year appointment had expired, and they hired C.H. Robinson, who had directed the college division during the administration of Joe Grant.

Students were not immediately affected by any of this. Instruction in the high school continued and a few hires were made in order to bolster the corps of teachers.

�«

Luis Torres, from Black Lake, graduated in 1959.

Luis is the younger brother of Indalesio, Manuel, and Robert, all of whom we have mentioned previously. A member of the Torres family had been at the school for twelve years continuously since 1947.

Luis grew up in Black Lake, as his brothers had, and he attended elementary school there to grade six. Luis boarded a bus daily to Eagle Nest for seventh and eighth grades. Luis spoke about the relative isolation that he experienced in Black Lake, there being no girls, for instance. Some of his relatives, Lourdes, Celedón, and Andrellita Espinoza attended the Normal School.

About the Normal School at El Rito, Luis told me, "I loved it the day I got there, the day I left, and I still like to go there." This in spite of the fact that students' social life had been lessened, movies on Sunday night had been discontinued, and students' social life involved athletic events and school dances.

Again, the "outside world" had little effect on him, and his teachers did not seem particularly worldly.

Luis took great interest in schoolmates, and he was particularly attentive to members of the class of 1959. Luis and I shared in a similar experience: Luis was elected president of his class each year in grades ten, eleven, and twelve, he told me. We talked about having become immersed in campus life at the expense of almost all else.

Luis mentioned to me that, although the school served him well in many ways, academically it did not. He said, "That may have been of my own doing." I doubt this, in viewing this thoughtful man in whom this trait has not changed.

Students, in Luis's memory, were not critical of anything, room or food or any living condition. "We were happy there," he nodded with finality. Leaving the Normal School upon graduation left him with a sense of loss.

Luis commented that the institution "was remiss in not reminding students that they were hosted by the people of El Rito," as we discussed the frequent neglect of day students at the school.

Luis Torres is to this day very socially aware. He does community organizing in pursuit of worthy projects and causes, as a man of the people.

Luis resides in Española.

◻

The class of 1959 included several bright, conscientious students. Two come to mind immediatey: Cecilia Romero, from Peñasco, was class valedictorian. Mary Martha Martínez, from El Guique, was salutatorian.

◻

Again in 1959, the El Rito Eagles won the state schoolboys' basketball championship. A trio of boys, Ralph Martínez, Randy

Velarde, and Sam Martínez were back for their senior year, by now experienced and showing great polish in the way they played ball. Ralph and Randy were members of the state championship team of 1957 and they looked the part. They were joined by Sam, Gilbert Valdez, Cándido Trujillo, Arthur Martínez, Carlos Martínez, Pablo Maestas, and Sifredo Martínez in rounding out another fine team coached by Vince Martínez. The 1959 Eagles breezed through a season, followed by district and regional tournaments, posting a record of 31 wins and two losses on their way to the state championship. The El Rito Eagles beat a good team from San Jon in the state finals, 55 to 45.

El Rito dominated the all-state team with three members: Ralph Martínez, Randy Velarde, and Sam Martínez.

◻

In summer, 1959, following graduation of the high school class, C.H. Robinson recommended a change in the name of the school to Northern New Mexico College, which the Board of Regents adopted. This was Robinson's courageous attempt to maintain the academic nature of the school's program, and to reinitiate a training program for the preparation of teachers.

Letter "N" Club was always a source of pride for lettermen and an informal forum for social discourse. In 1951 members included in the Bottom row: Pete Lobato, Cipriano Romero, Benito Juárez, Leonard Trujillo, Danny Chávez, Tony Montoya, Joe Jaramillo, Ray Sánchez, Billy Vigil, and Joe García. Middle row: Eloy Abeyta, Fred Mares, Arthur Martínez, Salomon Jaramillo, Joe Fernández, Alex García, and Regino Salazar. Top row: Sammy Sánchez, David García, Abel Gómez, and Charlie Aragón.

The El Rito Eagles captured the district football championship in 1954. Pictured are Top row: Mike Jaramillo, Eligio Jaramillo, Lupe Juárez, Michael Branch, Salomon Archuleta, Oscar Saiz, John Cosby, Eli Valdez, Ted Martínez, and Ray Esquibel. Middle row: Coach Vince Martínez, Orlando Dow, Bernie Lucero, Estolano Márquez, Leroy Martínez, M.R. Goode, Richard García, Joe Valdez, David Borunda, and Coach Frank Byers. Bottom row: Richard Riley, Horace Roybal, Johnny Sánchez, Albert Esparcen, Sammy Esquibel, Dennis Salazar, Leroy Martínez, and Amarante Sánchez.

The track team in 1954 was made up of Top row: David Borunda, Oscar Saiz, Lupe Juárez, and Orlando Dow. Bottom row: Michael Branch, Ted Martínez, and Estolano Márquez. Ted was an outstanding sprinter, and an avid student of the sport. Ted, Estolano, Lupe, and Albert Esparcen (not pictured) competed in sprint relays.

Lupe Juárez (shown left) and Joe Martínez were two of the finest high school athletes to play ball in New Mexico. In this 1954 photograph, they are shown in uniform with their favorite numbers, which the school should have retired. Lupe was an all around athlete who starred in basketball, football, and baseball. But his fame was achieved in football as the Normal School's only first-team high school All-American, as pass-receiving end. Joe Martínez, although not a big man by today's reckoning, was one of the most exciting basketball forwards to play the game.

The junior class in 1955 listed its officers. Sitting front row: Reyna Velarde, treasurer; Olivia Salazar, secretary; Estolano Márquez, president; Sabine Griego, vice president; Isaura Maes, student council representative; and Lydia Jaramillo (not shown), reporter. Standing back row are Reuben Rose, class sponsor; Johnny Sánchez, student council representative; Orlando Dow, sergeant-at-arms; and Humberto Gurulé, class sponsor.

In 1955, the cheerleading squad, beginning at top, were Patsy Trujillo, Sylvia Lucero, Olivia Salazar, Louise Archuleta, and Alicia Valdez.

Sophomore class officers in 1955 were (sitting left to right) Phil Miera, student council representative; Sigfredo Maestas, president; Otilia "Tillie" Esquibel, secretary-treasurer; and Connie Valdez, student council representative. Not shown is Leo García, vice president. Standing are Mr. Glenn George and Mr. Edward Grant, class sponsors.

In 1957, freshmen class officers were (sitting left to right) Erlinda Gonzáles, vice president; Beatrice López, secretary; and Pancha Martínez, treasurer. Standing are Joe Valdez, sergeant-at-arms and Bernard Montoya, president.

Girls' Athletic Association (GAA) was one of the more popular athletic and social activities in 1957. Although the photograph used for this book has no legend with it, we include it for its large number of students. Members who are identifiable include, in the top row, Pancha Martínez, Patsy Esquibel and Lucille Gonzáles among the first three and Virginia Archuleta (extreme right.) Second row from top: Rosalie Montoya, Ida Montoya, Cecilia Romero and Cecilia Archuleta (extreme right.) Third row includes Suzie Martínez and Polly Abeyta (first two on left.) Fourth row from the top: Laura Padilla, Erlinda Gonzáles, Cecilia Gonzáles, Laura López and Servilia Baca (second, fourth, fifth, sixth, and eighth from left.) Bottom row: Mae Rose Maestas, Martha Córdova, Mary Branch, Beatrice López, Martha Martínez, Nila Jaramillo, Nancy Zamora, Armida Velarde, Virginia García, unidentified, Lydia Archuleta, and Lugie Roseanne Martínez. Club sponsor on the far left is Ms. Bernie Trujillo. Armida Velarde was the association president. (Names to include on an errata page are invited.)

Sophomore class officers in 1957 were (sitting left to right) Luis Torres, vice president; Martha Martínez, secretary; and Gilbert García, treasurer. Standing: Adolfo Manzanares, president; Ms. Consuelo Torres, class sponsor; Louie Vigil, sergeant-at-arms; and Mr. Dan Trujillo, class sponsor.

The 1957 state champion El Rito Eagles were one of the finest high school basketball teams to have played ball in New Mexico, rivaled principally by the 1959 Eagles, who also won the state title and included a core of these same athletes. From left to right in the picture are Vince Martinez, coach; Albert Sánchez, Chris Quintana, David Valdez, Ralph Martínez, Dennis Branch, Randy Velarde, Porfirio Sánchez, Sam Martínez, Johnny Jaramillo, Joseph Valdez, and Richard Manzanares, manager.

8

THE FINAL DECADE OF THE NORMAL SCHOOL began
with hope on the part of those in charge of the school that not only
might the high school program be saved, but that they would guide
the school to achieve congruence with its original mission. That is,
that a junior college that offered preparatory courses for potential
public school teachers would be viewed approvingly by the Board of
Educational Finance, the governor, and the legislature.

Children of the Normal School, in 1960, viewed their school
differently. Not knowing about sentiments to eliminate the high school
that the school's administration was combating, students continued to
be steeped in the tradition of their school. Witness the fact that in 1960
El Chamisal referred to Northern New Mexico Normal School, in spite
of the fact that the name had not been recognized by state officials for
about four years.

◙

The class of 1960 included Erlinda Gonzáles, from Roy, who
was class valedictorian; and Lorraine Vigil, a student from El Rito, who
was salutatorian.

◙

The spotlight on sports changed from team to individual sports
during the 1960s. With the arrival of Ruben Lucero as coach, the school
began to achieve prominence in track and cross-country. Lucero also
assisted Marty with basketball and football, but it was in cross-country,
particularly, that Lucero's program excelled.

◙

Gerry García, easily the most widely known athlete to have attended the Normal School and an outstanding runner, began competing in invitational meets as early as seventh grade, and he began to compete for the high school in eighth grade. He chuckled as he said to me, "Ruben Lucero discovered me."

Gerry dominated cross-country in New Mexico throughout the first half of this decade, by winning the state championship in this sport five times consecutively. For this reason, we'll weave Gerry's story into the remaining narrative of the school up to 1965.

He attracted attention early on as a small boy when people saw him running, in preference to walking, around El Rito. Gerry would go out on the track field, occasionally, to watch Sofío his brother, and other boys on the track team. As the other boys grew to know Gerry, they marveled that he would run everywhere without seeming to tire.

Sofío invited his little brother to compete in a meet in Los Lunas while Gerry was in seventh grade, where Gerry managed to beat an older boy who had been state class B champion.

The El Rito Eagles won the state cross-country championship for the first time in 1961. Cross-country was a relatively new interscholastic sport. Gerry García, who finished first in the state class B division as an eighth grader, ran the course in 11 minutes and six seconds (11:06), fully 36 seconds faster than the state champ had run in the previous year.

Gerry had plenty of competition from his own team, however. Sam Archuleta, from Truchas, finished the course in 11:10 for the Eagles. El Rito had become a powerhouse in cross-country; the 1961 team included William Gonzáles, Billy Trujillo, Tito Ortiz, and Chris Martínez, in addition to Sam and Gerry.

The following year, 1962, Gerry García, with a time of 10:57, repeated as state champion. Sam Archuleta placed third. The Eagles were repeat champions in the state meet.

◙

María Dolores Gonzáles was of the graduating class of 1963. María Dolores, whom I interviewed for this book, is one of three sisters from Roy, out in the *llano* of New Mexico, where local folks speak English as cowboys do.

The three girls were close in age: Erlinda was born in 1942, Cecilia in 1944, and María Dolores in 1946. You met Erlinda briefly, as the top student of the class of 1960.

I appreciated the quiet pride that María Dolores has in her sisters' accomplishments and her own. The cultural isolation in which Hispanic children would grow up in Roy may be difficult to understand in northern New Mexico, but it wore on the three girls. They were fortunate to be guided by their mother, an elementary school teacher in a one-room schoolhouse. The girls also had their father, but he moved about in his job. The Gonzáles sisters started school in Roy with nuns, but then attended grades one to eight in Rosebud.

María Dolores recalled that when Erlinda completed eighth grade at Rosebud, she had to make a decision about high school, where to attend. Francis Gonzáles, an uncle, was newly graduated from college and he was slated to begin a teaching career at Northern New Mexico Normal School. Erlinda elected to attend the Normal School, thereby giving Cecilia, who was only eleven or twelve years of age, reason to attend the Normal School, also. The year was 1956, and Erlinda and Cecilia headed for El Rito. Erlinda enrolled in ninth grade, Cecilia in seventh.

María Dolores Gonzáles's picture appears in the 1959–1960 issue of *El Chamisal*; she was in ninth grade.

María Dolores described several parallels in the sisters' lives, activities, and successes. They all three were cheerleaders in a remarkably close school environment in which athletic and related activities were important to students. María Dolores was also a class vice-president, and in her senior year she edited *El Aguila*, the student newspaper.

The three sisters did well academically, although María Dolores commented that the school was not exceptionally strong in this way. Erlinda, I mentioned earlier, was class valedictorian in 1960; María Dolores was class salutatorian in 1963, as her sister Cecilia had been in 1962.

Erlinda, Cecilia, and María Dolores each received scholarships after high school in order to attend the University of New Mexico.

For a while, Erlinda taught in California, before returning to UNM for her master's and doctoral degrees. She subsequently taught in Indiana and at New Mexico State University, before returning to the University of New Mexico on its faculty in the department of modern foreign languages. She has resided in Oregon where she has been on the faculty of the University during the past few years.

Cecilia attended the University of New Mexico for two years. She then transferred to New Mexico Highlands University where she obtained bachelor's and master's degrees in bilingual education. Cecilia's career in education was in Colorado and New Mexico. Cecilia resides in Albuquerque.

María Dolores began studies at the University of New Mexico, married while in college, and then attended Adams State University in Colorado, where she obtained a bachelor's degree. She returned to UNM where she earned master's and doctoral degrees in socio-linguistics.

She has been on the faculty of the University of New Mexico. At present, she is executive director of a company, Bilingual Strategies, which offers training for business executives in language, translation, mediation, and cultural competency.

Since 2010, María Dolores Gonzáles has been president of the Normal School Alumni Association the past two years.

María Dolores resides in Albuquerque.

◲

Sam Archuleta graduated at the Normal School in 1964.

Sam was a boy from Truchas, a rural village in the western foothills of the Sangre de Cristo mountains. He was an excellent athlete, placing in state cross-country meets two years, as I have recounted.

Sam was a good student. Following high school he obtained degrees in business and in law. He operates a business in Albuquerque, offering services as an attorney and as a certified public accountant.

Sam was president of the Normal School Alumni Association when I met him.

◙

In 1964, Gerry García was a seasoned athlete in cross-country, although still in eleventh grade. He repeated as state champion for the fourth consecutive time. In 1964, the state had divided schools into three classes for competition: AA, A, and B. El Rito competed again in class B, and Gerry posted a new time of 9:32 for the same course, faster than boys from Sandía and Los Lunas High Schools, in classes AA and A, respectively.

◙

The graduating class of 1964 numbered forty students, fairly large for the Normal School. Numbers for enrollment in the remaining years of the high school would get smaller.

This class included a few familiar faces, students whom I got to know long after they and I had graduated at the Normal School: John Dantis, Mary Agnes Griego, Oliver Vigil, Sam Archuleta, Napoleon Quintana, and Arturo Sisneros.

Maxine Gallegos, from La Madera was class valedictorian; Tom Martin, El Rito, was salutatorian.

◙

The Normal School also enjoyed successes in track. In 1964, the mile relay team, coached by Ruben Lucero, won district and conference championships. This four-man team included Sam Archuleta, Billy Trujillo, Billy Jaramillo, and William Gonzáles.

The mile medley-relay team was made up of Ben Cordova, Dave Padilla, Sam Archuleta, and Gerry García. This team held the school record.

◙

Beginning with the school year 1958–1959, C.H. Robinson and the administrative staff had tried to promote the idea of a new school, Northern New Mexico College, and to develop its junior college program. After some initial enthusiasm on the part of the Board of

Regents, opposition mounted as the governor and legislature in Santa Fé became more interested in vocational education, and they opposed the junior college that Robinson favored. In June 1964, Charles H. Robinson resigned as president after a courageous effort of six years as head of the school.

Lito Martínez was hired as the new superintendent. He took two actions early on that met with the approval of the school's new Board of Regents and their funding agency, the Board of Educational Finance. He resumed the use of the name Northern New Mexico State School in the school's communications, and he hired a staff to plan a vocational education program.

▣

Pauline Alire graduated with the class of 1965.

Pauline began school in Placitas in 1954 when Max Varoz was principal of the elementary school. Several of her school's teachers were graduates of the old Normal School.

In 1961, Pauline enrolled in high school at the Normal School. She remembered two of her favorite teachers at the time, Albert Jenske and Gilbert Vigil.

It was important to prepare to go to work after high school, Pauline told me. Parents were neither able nor inclined to send their daughters to college. Pauline enrolled at the New Mexico Technical Vocational School where she prepared to do office work, little realizing what the future would have in store. She remembered, as we spoke, Priscilla Trujillo, and excellent instructor in some of her classes. She also recalled fondly Drucilla Duran and Martha Salazar.

Pauline Alire Varoz became secretary to the president when I came to Northern New Mexico Community College in the latter capacity in January 1985. Pauline continued on as secretary to the president, after I left, until her retirement.

Pauline, Lucas Trujillo, and Juan García have constituted the nucleus of the board of the El Rito Water Users' association, a great service to the community and to the college.

Pauline and her husband, Larry Varoz, reside in El Rito.

The 1965 track team included three very well-conditioned young athletes: Gerry García, Ben Trujillo, and Billie Trujillo. I interviewed the first two of these men for this book.

Ben Trujillo, a boy from El Rito, was in the class of 1965.

Ben was the son of Aniceta Trujillo—she was known in the community as Annette—and the grandson of Jeronimo Jaramillo. As a note of explanation, although Venceslao Jaramillo, the founder of the Normal School, did not leave any direct descendants, Ben and Annette and a cousin by the name of Guadalupita Jaramillo were among known relatives of Venceslao.

Ben started elementary school at the Normal with a pre-first teacher, Lola Valdez, who lived across from the campus and whom people in El Rito still remember. For second grade, Ben had Mela Leger as his teacher. Ben remembered how very much he enjoyed elementary school and that he had several good teachers, two of whom I've named, but there were more whose names he could not remember.

In high school, things were different. Ben stated things were not as "normal" as one would like. Water quality was not good, there being sediments perceptible in every glass of water. Substitute facilities had to be sought for an aging Junior Building. The school brought in a set of barracks.

Ben liked all of his schoolmates and remembered especially Chris Martínez, Leroy Salazar, Angela Bertha Trujillo, Gerry García, Forencio Archuleta, Rudy Martínez, and Tito Ortíz.

Ben was very complimentary of teachers and staff, including students who worked at the school. He singled out Dennis Salazar as having been especially helpful. In high school, Melvin Cordova, whom he also liked, was principal. He praised Ruben Lucero for his guidance as coach for track, basketball, and football. He remembered having given his coach a western-style belt buckle as a gift.

Ben was pleased about the education that he received at the high school. His parents, who were educated people, insisted that he continue on to college after high school, which he did.

After college, Ben became a businessman and business consultant. Ben lived and worked in Denver, during which time he commuted to El Rito to visit his mother.

Ben Trujillo had been living in Santa Fé with his wife when in winter 2010 he died in a tragic accident.

◙

Gerry García graduated with the class of 1966.

Records that he set at the Normal School remain indelible. In the fall of 1965, Gerry won a fifth consecutive state title in cross-country in a time of 9:41. His winning time was 34 seconds faster than the class A winner, and eight seconds under the time of the class AA champion, boys from Silver City and Hobbs, respectively.

Gerry's records at the school were never erased, because a few years later, in 1969, his school was closed. More important, however, is the fact that winning the state championship five years consecutively is so difficult to achieve that the odds that someone will surpass Gerry García's accomplishments are miniscule. And in the nation, there are two boys who have won state competitions four times. No one that I know about has won consecutively beginning with eighth grade.

Gerry likes to poke fun at himself. He mentioned to me that Ruben Lucero, his coach, lived on the side of the campus nearest the elementary school where Gerry attended. He said Ruben had seen him one day "showing off" his running ability. It would be the beginning of a long and close friendship between Gerry and his coach. He said that both Ruben Lucero and his wife provided encouragement to him throughout his career at the Normal School.

After high school, Coach Lucero and his wife drove Gerry to Portales and Eastern New Mexico University. Ruben Lucero had introduced Gerry to Coach Carl Babcock, who, in turn, offered Gerry a scholarship at Eastern. During his time at Eastern, Coach Babcock provided Gerry "with the structure to succeed."

In Portales, Gerry excelled again in cross-country, winning fourth place in a field of 320 runners in the National Collegiate

Association (NCAA) meet held in Wheaton, Illinois. He was named All-American in 1966, and he received the "Greatest Grayhound" award at Eastern New Mexico University in 1967.

Gerry García transferred to Lamar University when Coach Babcock left Eastern to coach at the east Texas school. He had developed a very high regard for Babcock, who entered him the following year in the Texas Relays in the 10,000 meter run. Gerry managed to finish second to Jack Bachelor, a superb runner, and he beat Frank Shorter, whom track enthusiasts will remember as an Olympic champion who lived in Taos.

Gerry was determined to one day beat both great runners in competition. In an AAU meet he ran a mile in 4:18 to get ahead of Bachelor and Shorter, only to injure a calf-muscle. He was forced to give up the race.

He emphasized throughout our discussion that two things were important to him: doing his personal best always, and demonstrating loyalty to his former coaches.

Gerry also said to me, "I owe a lot to Ruben. He was my coach for five years." Ruben Lucero and Carl Babcock turned out to be great influence in Gerry's life as an athlete.

Carl Babcock, about whom he thinks often, died during Gerry's college career.

Gerry and his wife have taught in the Albuquerque Public Schools. He and his wife and young daughter live in Albuquerque.

Seeking new challenges, Gerry is enrolling in a doctoral program at the University of New Mexico in school administration and special education.

◻

The class of 1969 knew that the high school would close at the end of the school year. Teachers made certain that students enjoyed their stay during that final year. The staff supported all of the usual activities: student government, boys basketball and track, cheering squad, and class activities.

The New Mexico Technical Vocational School had been

planned by administration, and changes on campus were visible. Most evident to students was that there was now a different yearbook in 1969, *El Paisano*. The graduating class numbered only 19; there were almost no boarding students left.

The remainder of the high school had 22 students in eleventh grade, 21 sophomores, and 26 in ninth grade. In order for these students to continue their studies, they would likely enroll in the Mesa Vista High School, down the road in Ojo Caliente.

▣

In the high school, honor students were Greg Martin, Anthony Manzanares, Isabel Vigil, and Richard Romero

Greg Martin, class of 1969, was the last of the Martins to attend the Normal School. Greg is Tom Martin's son, and the grandson of George J. Martin. Greg has a brother Tom and sister Cam who also attended the Normal School. Tom was a music teacher in the Albuquerque Public Schools. He resides in Albuquerque. Cam lives in Taos.

Greg was born in 1952 and began school in El Rito on the campus of the Normal School. Soon thereafter, he attended St. Thomas Elementary School in Abiquiú in grades two to eight.

Greg came to the Normal School for ninth grade, where he excelled academically and in school athletics. He lettered in all four sports, baseball, basketball, football, and track. From the time he entered high school, Anthony Manzanares from Los Ojos and Patrick Barela from Peñasco were his friends.

When Greg came to the school, Melvin Cordova was principal; Vince Martínez and Ruben Lucero coached the sports program, and John Romero was music director.

After high school, Greg enrolled at the University of New Mexico. With academic interests similar to his grandfather's, George Martin, Greg enrolled in the University in order to study languages. Greg is fluent in Spanish and English, more and more a rarity even in New Mexico.

As a student in latin american studies at the University, Greg enrolled in the University's Andean Studies Center in Quito, Ecuador. He furthered his language studies, in Portuguese and in Quechua, the language of the indigenous people of the highlands of South America.

Greg returned from South America to El Rito to assist the family after his father had become ill.

In January 1974, Greg took over the operation of the Martin store, established by George J. Martin a half century earlier.

Greg and his wife Josie reside in El Rito.

◙

The high school that had emerged out of the old Spanish American Normal School, fifty years earlier, closed its doors with graduation of the class of 1969.

The Northern New Mexico College band in 1961 was led by music instructor John Romero, who had a long tenure at the school and was beloved by his students. This year's band included, in the First row, Marcia Valdez, Johnell Carlson, Barbara García, Barbara Valdez, Alonzo García, Davie Padilla, Alfonso Trujillo, Silviano Archuleta, Jerry Branch, Theresa Lobato, Nickie Dantis, John Dantis, Sally Archuleta, and Rudy Maestas. Second row: Pat Nieto, Tommy Martin, Esther Sánchez, Mary Agnes Griego, Amabel Gonzáles, and Rosie Quintana. In the back row, Band Director John Romero, David Valdez, John Griego, Cecilia García, John Lucero, Benny Trujillo, Presy Archuleta, Wenona Sloan, Ray Sloan, Maryann Sánchez, Tony Márquez, and John Romero. Photo is from *El Chamisal*.

The 1961 Student Council members were, Front row left to right, Cecilia Gonzáles, vice president; Cam Martin, secretary; Julian Padilla, president; Pat Nieto, treasurer; and Bobby Romero, parliamentarian. Middle row: Priscilla Carrillo, Roberta Orona, Rosie Quintana, Cecilia García, Gladys Archuleta, and Nancy Martínez. Back row: Milnor Branch, Leo Estrada, Orlando Lucero, Amelia Vigil, Sifredo Martínez, and Mr. Al Jenschke, council sponsor. Photo is from *El Chamisal*.

TRACK TEAM OF '63

Track and cross-country developed into the strongest programs in the Normal School's history under the tutelage of Coach Ruben Lucero. The number of boys on the 1963 track team provide evidence of this; shown in the photograph are Frank Perea, Leroy Zamora, Rudy Martínez, Carlos Martínez, Tito Ortíz, Fabián Martínez, William Gonzáles, Billy Trujillo, Dave Padilla, Gerry García, Ben Córdova, James Baca, Chris Martínez, Sam Archuleta, Richard Velásquez, Coach Lucero, Joe Córdova, John Dantis, Leroy Salazar, Billy Jaramillo, Gilbert López, and Nappy Quintana. Photo taken from a 1964 *El Chamisal.*

Students took their governance seriously. Student Council members in 1963 included, sitting from left to right, Ronald Valdez, Leroy Salazar, Dorothy Martínez, Treasurer Cecilia García, President Dolores Gonzáles, Vice President Gladys Archuleta, Marcia Valdez, and Robert Rivera. Additional members include Arthur Sisneros, Cordy Varoz, Agusta García, David Rotering, Mike Salazar, David Valdez, Billy Jaramillo, William Gonzáles, Council Sponsor Al Jenschke, Maxine Gallegos, Cecilia Martínez. Not shown is Sandra Gonzáles.

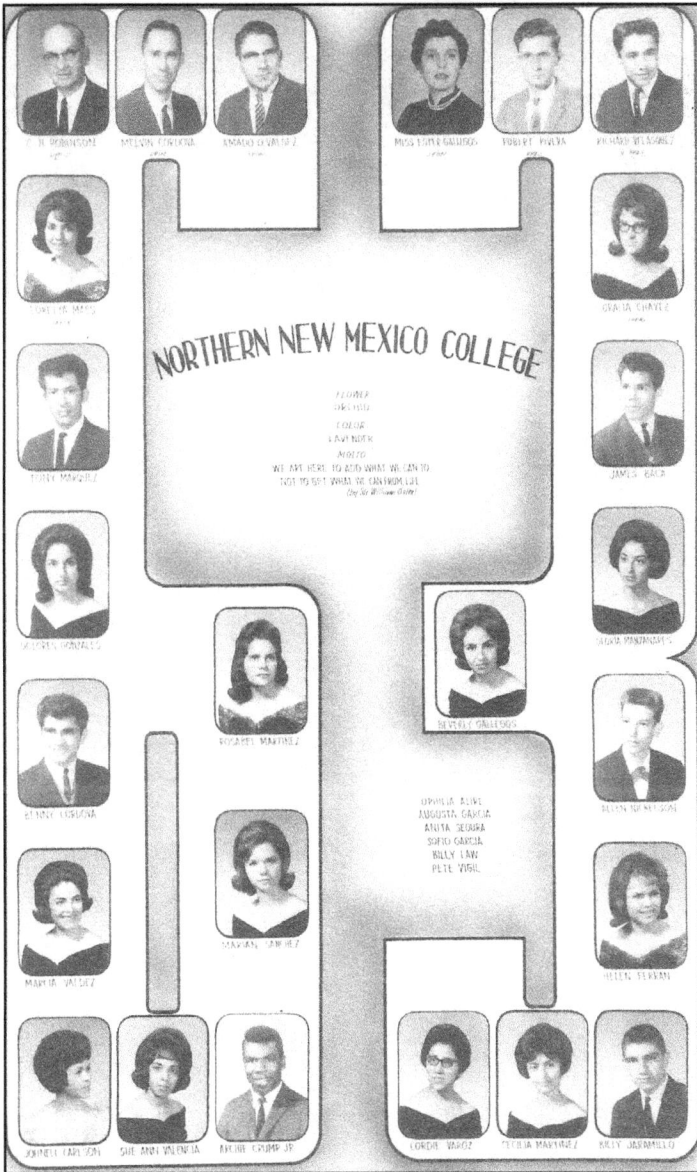

The graduating class of 1963 continued the use of an idea that gave rise a couple of years earlier to picture posters of their classmates. Also in the picture are Charles H. Robinson, top left, and the high school principal Melvin Córdova, second from left. The fourth person in the left hand column is María Dolores Gonzáles, the president of the Normal School Alumni Association this year. The few remaining records of this type may be found in the Office of the President, Northern New Mexico College.

The 1965 track team honored its top runners in this 1965 photograph. Left to right are Gerry García, Billy Trujillo, and Benny Trujillo. Photograph taken from a 1966 *El Chamisal*.

Three members of El Rito's marching band were named to All State Band: Joe García and David Jarmillo, trumpeters, and Richard García, clarinetist.

During sixty years of the Spanish American Normal School and its successors, life for the Children of the Normal School had changed markedly.

In the early years of the Spanish American Normal School, students lived within the Spanish and Mexican cultures that their parents had known, left after the occupation of New Mexico by Spain in the late sixteenth century and by Mexico since 1821. In 1969, those old times were a subject for the history books. The most profound difference between new and old was the means by which people communicated. Spanish as the dominant language had given way to English. The old language was used only in informal conversation; all formal discourse was now in English. The occupation of this region by the United States of America became a decisive triumph, socially, culturally, and linguistically, for all intents and purposes during the lifetime of the Children of the Normal School.

Children of the Normal School were patriots, staunch in their belief in the democratic ideals of this country. Witness, for example, our behavior during the 1960s, a period of unrest in the US owing to issues like civil rights and the Nation's involvement in the Vietnam War. Young people in this part of the world were vitally interested in the civil rights of all minority individuals, but believed in non-violent means of achieving ends, as espoused by Dr. Martin Luther King, perhaps. Even those who disagreed with the US involvement in Vietnam subscribed to the notion that this was "my country, right or wrong." I speak here about what seemed to me to be the prevailing opinion among us.

Technology influenced the new way of life, in welcome fashion. The road leading to the campus was far better; vehicles abounded; and electricity, permitting the use of radio, telephones, and television, was present in every corner of the county.

National and cultural news were first formally disseminated in English by the *Santa Fe New Mexican*, a newspaper to which only a few people subscribed. In October 1956, the *Río Grande Sun* was established by Robert Trapp in Española, increasing people's awareness and interest in local news. Seven years later, in 1963, KDCE became the first radio station in our midst, although two popular stations had existed earlier in Santa Fé.

One might lament the loss of our earlier isolation, but one has to ponder about how the minds, hopes, aspirations, and dreams of young people were affected in ways that might matter because of that condition. It is very little wonder that the "sense of loss," summarized by Luis Torres, as we spoke in preparation of this book, has been expressed in one way or another by the Children of the Normal School in differing ways through the years. Although we were young, our behavior offered a glimpse into a community with a culture of its own. The Children of the Normal spoke their own language, as young people everywhere are apt to do, but moreover they stressed their own values. Although probably no more virtuous than any other group of people, the Children of the Normal School nevertheless maintained their informal rules of behavior, always in line with the social mores that they had learned back home. In summary, if schools are successful in socializing young people, then the Normal School was greatly more successful in providing its Children with a set of principles that would sustain them. This they achieved almost entirely on their own.

◻

The institution that began as the Spanish American Normal School, which is remembered by Children of the Normal School as their high school, requires a postscript.

Many former students wonder simply, "¡Qué pasó?" Why did this wonderful little school that harbored me during some important years of my life finally close? Weren't there many more kids, especially in this day and age, who needed refuge in this wonderful place in which to grow up? With all of this discussion in our state and nation about the underachievement of students, wasn't there a continuing need for this school? Change like this makes no sense to me.

In the previous paragraph, I paraphrase many of our thoughts. I'll summarize briefly, what did happen?

Venceslao Jaramillo could foresee much more than anyone knew, or that is appreciated today. Northern New Mexico deeply needed a school in which to train teachers. Because of his political knowledge and ability, as I have explained early in this book, he was able to establish, with the help of L. Bradford Prince and his Republican friends, the Spanish American Normal School at El Rito.

People up here, in our hills and valleys, weren't ready for this type of instruction, so the school took the next logical step. It began elementary and high school instruction for prospective teachers, and anyone else who would attend. In time, we, who were "anyone else," far outnumbered students who came to study to become teachers. Our preeminence grew as a high school, not least for the attributes that I have described, including our high school's prowess in interscholastic sports.

The state's political will to continue the Normal School was present with Republicans up until they were displaced by Democrats at the state capital in the early thirties. This willingness by the state to support the high school continued until 1951 when Joseph B. Grant was replaced as head of the school. And then, political will started to wane. The Normal School was, after all, supported by New Mexico's taxpayers, and state politicians began to question the efficacy of maintaining the school. Since the departure of Joe Grant no single politician has been sufficiently interested, or powerful, to argue for the *status quo* at El Rito.

Since the high school' closing in 1969, the institution has been the subject of a number of experiments, some sound and some not, described for readers in the next chapter, its epilogue.

9

IN THIS BRIEF EPILOGUE WE'LL SUMMARIZE what has happened to the Normal School since 1969.

Readers may recall the formation of the New Mexico Technical Vocational School. This action resulted from pressure from the Governor's office and the Board of Educational Finance that the Board of Regents found difficult to resist, perhaps out of weariness.

To review further, the Board in 1958 had resolved to create a junior college program to be run in conjunction with the high school, and it employed Charles H. Robinson to develop the two-year college program and to begin its operation. Robinson did what he had been hired to do. He had the needed experience—he was registrar at New Mexico Highlands University—and the desire to assist the Normal School in the preparation of teachers, as was intended by the founders of the school. This model for the operation of the Normal School had been tried before, during the administration of John V. Conway in the early 1930s, and again by Joseph B. Grant and C.H. Robinson in the forties.

The Board of Regents had to succumb, unfortunately, to the wishes of those who determined funding for the school. Northern New Mexico College, as Robinson and the Regents had named it, had not had sufficient time to build its student enrollment. The high school still distinguished itself for its ability to attract students, a situation that state officials did not want.

Politicians sometimes promulgate concepts and ideas that are made of dreams and create false expectations, which is what happened in this case. The new line—declared without careful study—was that northern New Mexico should train its young people for jobs, and thus was formulated the New Mexico Technical Vocational School.

回

No one bothered to point out that the Vocational School would limit access to only one type of education for which there might not be sufficient jobs in the region. For example, it would not prepare students for jobs in science or engineering, nor for executive positions, if opportunities should arise in their workplace. Add to these a whole list of fields of study that the Vocational School would not offer.

Student enrollment in the New Mexico Technical Vocational School was satisfactory, given the fact that the GI Bill and other financial aid became available for students to attend school. The administration at El Rito saw opportunity to expand its programs into Española, and it did with the concurrence of the Board of Regents.

Expansion into the Española valley, more than any other initiative, gave rise to other ideas among young people only informally associated with the school. Community members in close contact with Dennis Salazar and other members of the Board of Regents—Dennis chaired the Board—urged officials of the school to create a community college. Two presidents of the Vocational School, Alex Mercure and Frank Serrano, assisted the Board in preparing to accomplish the school's next change in mission.

After only eight years, in 1977, the school came to be known as Northern New Mexico Community College.

回

The community college was able to continue to teach vocational education and it offered a full academic program typical of a junior college, by subsuming a two-year college program offered by the University of New Mexico in this north central region. The community college, in addition, offered art, folk arts, and cultural and entertainment courses, along with courses designed to help working people in their jobs and careers. In a word, the community college offered a vast array of courses to suit almost anyone's need.

In the nineties, Northern New Mexico Community College started offering professional training programs for teachers.

I became president of the school a second time in 1996 when, by the new millennium, the Community College began to offer coursework that would permit a student who already possessed the baccalaureate degree to certify as a teacher by taking the professional, i.e. education, courses at Northern New Mexico Community College.

Evidence began to mount in the earliest years of the new century that public schools in our region were having difficulty finding teachers whom to hire. A shortage of qualified teachers was projected into another decade. We can say safely now that this was not a false alarm, and, in fact, a shortage of trained teachers continues.

In 2002 and 2003, we began to explore whether Northern New Mexico Community College should expand its charge by beginning to offer the bachelor's degree in teacher education, namely elementary, secondary, and special education. The notion was, and continues to be, congruent with the founding legislation of the Spanish American Normal School. We requested, with concurrence by the Board of Regents, that our legislators introduce the necessary legislation to ascertain the authority of Northern New Mexico Community College to offer this baccalaureate degree. The effort met with the near unanimous approval of the legislature.

Governor Richardson came to the campus, and before a full auditorium, signed Senate Bill 163 that said, in part, "The board of regents of northern new mexico state school is authorized to develop, implement and seek accreditation for a baccalaureate degree program in teacher education for the Española campus." The document goes on to say that the school may offer the program when it is accredited, and that the school shall engage New Mexico Highlands University as it proceeds with its offerings.

This historic event is commemorated in the signed bill on the 5th day of March 2004, witnessed by Diane D. Denish, President of the Senate, Ben Lujan, Speaker of the House of Representatives, and Margaret Larragoite and Stephen R. Arias, Chief Clerk of the Senate and House, respectively.

The Normal School had become the institution that was intended during its founding in 1909.

◻

I retired from Northern New Mexico Community College as its president in February 2005, but not before we had sought and obtained accreditation by the Higher Education Commission (North Central) for programs leading to the BA degree in elementary, secondary, and special education.

◻

One of the early actions of the school after I left was to change the name of the institution to Northern New Mexico College. José Griego was president and he requested that legislation be introduced to reflect the name change. A second change states that in its management and control of the school, the Board Regents shall be viewed in all respects in the same manner that the constitution of New Mexico deals with other state educational institutions mentioned in Article 12, Section 11, i.e., its universities.

Since July 1, 2005, the school has been officially known as Northern New Mexico College.

Bill Richardson is shown signing Senate Bill 163 during the afternoon on March 5, 2004, in a ceremony in the Nick L. Salazar Center for the Arts on the campus of Northern New Mexico Community College in Española. Witnessing signing of the bill, which authorizes the school to offer the baccalaureate degree in teacher education, are Regent Michael Branch, College President Sigfredo Maestas, Regent Levi Pesata (partially obscured), Regent Nelson Cournoyer, State Senator Richard Martínez, and State Representatives Debbie Rodella and Nick Salazar.

References

Only Yesterday, Frederick Lewis Allen (1931). Originally published by Harper and Row, Publishers, New York, NY, in 1931. My copy is one of the First Perennial Classics republished by Perennial Classics in 2000.

Romance of a Little Village Girl, Cleofas M. Jaramillo (1955). Originally published by The Naylor Company, San Antionio, TX, in 1955. My copy is by the University of New Mexico Press with a foreword by Tey Diana Rebolledo, a book in a series, *Pasó Por Aquí*, edited by Genaro M. Padilla, Erlinda Gonzáles-Berry, and A. Gabriel Meléndez.

Politics and Education in Hispanic New Mexico: From Spanish American Normal School to Northern New Mexico Community College, Guillermo Lux (1984), Northern New Mexico Community College, El Rito and Española, NM.

"Such, Such Were the Days," in *A Collection of Essays*, George Orwell (1946), Harcourt Publishing Company, USA .

Justice Betrayed, Ralph Melnick, University of New Mexico Press (2002).

Chili Line, John A. Gjevre, Río Grande Sun Press, Española, NM (1969, 1971).

Public School Education in New Mexico, Tom Wiley, Division of Government Research, The University of New Mexico (1965).

Interviews and Additional Reference material

David Grant, Albuquerque, September 18, 1997.

Gordon Darling, El Rito, summer 1998, and from his autobiography Chapter 5, copyright 1997.

John A. Martin, Santa Fé, February 2, 2007.

Jane Goddard García, El Rito, September 18, 2008.

Michael Branch, Santa Fé, September 24, 2008.

Roberta Brosseau, Santa Fé, January 29, 2009.

Dennis Salazar, Española, February 10, 2009.

Richard García, Santa Fé, February 12, 2009.

Lora Spaulding, Notre Dame University, telephone discussions and e-mails concerning Venceslao Jaramillo. February 12 & 13, 2009.

Angela Kindig, Notre Dame University, e-mail discussions concerning Venceslao Jaramillo. February 13 & 17, 2009.

Esperanza Baca Gonzáles, El Rito, February 13, 2009

George Luján, Española, February 13, 2009.

Jane Goddard García, El Rito, February 16, 2009.

Albert Esparcen, Santa Fé, February 24, 2009.

Michael Branch, Santa Fé, February 25, 2009.

Dana Allison and Katie Bateman Allison, winter and spring, 2009.

Meade Martin, March 2009, provided audiotapes that include a narration by Lawrence Redman.

Robert Torres, Española, March 4, 2009.

Elizabeth Cook, Regis College, telephone discussion and e-mail, concerning Venceslao Jaramillo. March 18, 2009.

Estolano Marquez, telephone discussions, spring 2009.

Robert Torres, Taos, March 17, 2009.

Allison Aragón, Charlie Aragón, and Tony García; Albuquerque; March 24, 2009.

Priscilla Trujillo Schafer, Albuquerque, April 13, 2009.

Ben Trujillo, Santa Fé, April 17, 2009.

Ted Martínez, Albuquerque, May 20, 2009.

Rubén Miera, Albuquerque, August 15, 2009.

Leo Apodaca, Danny Englebrecht and Ted Kuntz; Albuquerque; August 15, 2009.

Nick L. Salazar, Española, September 15, 2009.

Joann Martin, El Rito, September 15, 2009.

David Trujillo, Española, September 23, 2009.

Cloide Trujillo, Española, fall 2009.

Pat Vigil, Albuquerque, October 18, 2009.

Larry Purcell, by telephone, October, 2009.

Mike Martin, El Rito, October 28, 2009.

Hyda María Dougherty, Santa Fé, October 30, 2009.

Gilbert Archuleta, Española, October andNovember, 2009.

Luis Torres, Española, October 2, 2009.

Gerry García, Albuquerque, February 4, 2010.

Ross López, Española, spring 2010.

Juan García, El Rito, November 23, 2009 and January 13, 2010.

Lucas Trujillo, El Rito, January 13, 2010.

Pauline Alire Varoz, El Rito, January 13, 2010.

David Borunda, Santa Fé, January 15, 2010.

Greg Martin, El Rito, January 20, 2010.

Michael Redman, in Española by telephone, February 8, 2010.

María Dolores Gonzáles, Albuquerque, April 16, 2010.

David Borunda, Albuquerque, July 28, 2010.

Lupe Juárez, Albuquerque, January 15, 2011.

Lee Leyba, Albuquerque, June 16, 2011.

Betty Rose, Santa Fé, June 30, 2011

Appendices

Students Who Attended During the Earliest Years

1909–10

José R. López, age 19, El Rito
Manuel Trujillo, age 20, El Rito
Anastacio Trujillo, 21, El Rito
Gilberto Durán, 20, El Rito
Martín Suazo, 19, Tierra Amarilla
Tomás Chávez, 18, Tierra Amarilla
Fidel Jaramillo, 16, Vallecitos
Onesimo Chávez, 16, Vallecitos
Alberto Chávez, 19 Vallecitos
Tomás Martínez, 16, Ranchos de Taos
Albert Miller, 18, Taos
Venceslao Martínez, 20, Taos
Dixie Dixon, 13, El Rito
Carlos Gonzáles, 15, El Rito
Gretchen Dixon, 14, El Rito
Ralph Dixon, 15, El Rito
Mrs. Keller, 23, Monero
May Madole, 17, Venus
Belle Woods, 17, Pagosa Junction, CO
Lenora Woods, 19, Nutrias
Bertha Livesay 20, Golden
Marie Fleming, 28, El Rito
Lida Rowe, 34, Estancia

Lee Rowe, 14, Estancia
Lola Chávez, 17, El Rito
Ana Chávez, 14, El Rito
Bertha Forney, 30, Mountainair
Elizabeth Doane, 28, Roswell
Carmen Martínez, 14, Abiquiu
Amabilís Moya, 17, Coyote
Baselisa Márquez, 15, El Rito
Cleofas Martínez, 18, La Madera
Jesus M. Jaramillo, 59, El Rito
Juan García, 19, Ojo Caliente
Geronimo Archuleta, 17, El Rito
Socorro Chacón, 16, El Rito
Oscar Hoskins, 20, Frankfort, KY
Alfredo Salazar, 14, Chamita
Refugio Guillén, 24, Alcalde
Guadalupe Trujillo, 20, Ojo Caliente
Celestino Jaramillo, 17, El Rito
Pedro Martínez, 16, Alcalde
Amalia Martínez, 25, Velarde
Eli Martínez, 18, Tierra Amarilla
Marie Ferrán, 24, Gallina
Clotilde Ortíz, 25, Alcalde

1910–11

Alfredo Salazar, 15, Chamita
Ralph Dixon, 16, El Rito
Gretchen Dixon, 15, El Rito
Dixie Dixon, 15, El Rito
Manuel S. Trujillo, 18, El Rito
Carlos Gonzáles, 15, El Rito
José R. López, 19, El Rito
Lenora Woods, 19, Venus
Belle Woods, 17, Venus
Sarah Keller, 23, Venus
Julián Trujillo, 17, Ojo Caliente
Martín J. Suazo, 20, Park View
Amalia M. Rodríguez, 27, Velarde
Amalia Chávez, 15, Vallecitos
Onesimo Chávez, 17, Vallecitos
Nettie Wartembe, 47, Springer
Tomás Rivera, 25, El Rito
Celestino Jarmillo, 18, El Rito
Cleofes Martínez, 20, Ojo Caliente
Pablo Gallegos, 18, Ojo Caliente
William Gallegos, 16, Ojo Caliente
Alberto Chávez, 17, Vallecitos
Miguel A. Gallegos, 19, El Rito
Cristóbal Quintana, 17, Taos
José M. Quintana, 16 Taos
Sadie Pippin, 24, Santa Fé
Fidel Jaramillo, 16, Vallecitos
Marína Jaramillo, 14, Vallecitos
Anastacio Trujillo, 20, El Rito
Lorenzo Herrera, 17, Chamita
Tomás Martínez, 18, Ranchos de Taos
Celso E. Martínez, 23, Ranchos de Taos
Gilberto Durán, 23, El Rito
Emilio Salazar, 16, Park View
Clotilde Trujillo, 23, El Rito

Flavio Montoya, 28, Española
Ursulo Ortíz, 21, Chimayó
Bonifacio R. Martínez, 22, Chimayó
Ramón R. Quintana, 22, Santa Cruz
Juan B. García, 21, Ojo Caliente
Juan S. Rael, 20, Questa
J. Enrique Rael, 19, Questa
Praxedes Rael, 15, Questa
Epifanio Rivera, 14 Ojo Caliente
Preciliano Moya, 15, Abiquiú
Baselisa Márquez, 17, El Rito
Francisco Rivera, 19, El Rito
Francisco Vigil, 17, El Rito
José D. Trujillo, 16, El Rito
Eduardo Baros, 15, El Rito
Amalia Chávez, 25, Abiquiú
Refugio Guillén, 27, Alcalde
Senaidita Guillén, 16, Alcalde

1911–12

Ralph Dixon, 17, El Rito
Gretchen Dixon, 16, El Rito
Dixie Dixon, 15, El Rito
Rudy Jaramillo, 12, El Rito
Ciria Martínez, 15, El Rito
Clotilde Trujillo, 24, El Rito
Preciliano López 18, El Rito
Gusmán Martínez, 14, El Rito
Fabián Gonzáles, 20, El Rito
José R. López, 20, El Rito
Gerónimo Archuleta, 19, El Rito
Miguel Gallegos, 20, El Rito
Carlos Gonzáles, 15, El Rito
Sadie Pippin, 25, Santa Fé
Julián Trujillo, 18, Ojo Caliente

Pablo Gallegos, 19, Ojo Caliente
Cleofes Martínez, 21, Ojo Caliente
William Gallegos, 17, Ojo Caliente
Dionicio Sánchez, 16, Ojo Caliente
Manuel Griego, 17, Ojo Caliente
Guadalupe Trujillo, 22, Ojo Caliente
Juan Espinoza, 22, Chamita
Maximiliano Salazar, 18, Chamita
Alfredo Salazar, 15, Chamita
Serapio Herrera, 11, Chamita
Lorenzo Herrera, 18, Chamita
Augustín García, 22, Chamita
Germán Gallegos, 18, Chamita
Canuto Trujillo, 16, Chimayó
Nemecio Martínez, 21, Chimayó
Joseph McWilliams, 20, Tierra
    Amarilla
Katherine Martínez, 14, Tierra
    Amarilla
José M. Quintana, 18, Taos
Cristóbal Quintana, 17, Taos
Antonio Montoya, 22, Taos
Juan Cisneros, 19, Taos
Fares Martínez, 22, Taos
Eusebio Vigil, 19, Taos
Nepomuceno Vigil, 20, Taos
Marcos Pacheco, 16, Arroyo Seco
Onesimo Torres, 19, Arroyo Seco
Alberto Chávez, 18, Vallecitos
Fidel Jaramillo, 17, Vallecitos
Quirino Vargas, 12, Vallecitos
Onesimo Chávez, 18, Vallecitos
Amalia Chávez, 16, Vallecitos
Lucía Chávez, 13, Vallecitos
Josefina Chávez, 10, Vallecitos
José R. P. Martínez, 12, Cebolla
Joe T. Montaño, 22, Cebolla

Juan Rael, 21, Questa
J. Enrique Rael, 21, Questa
Esequiel Rael, 18, Questa
Praxedes Rael, 18, Questa
Bailón B. Montaño, 19, Pastura
Amado Martínez, 17, Velarde
José D. Velarde, 18, Velarde
Juan López, 17, Santa Cruz
Josefina López, 18, Santa Cruz
Regina López, 15, Santa Cruz
Matilde Martínez, 15, El Rito
Jesusita Gallegos, 18, Abiquiú

Graduates of the Normal School

1922

Laura Redman

1923

Glenn Redman
Sixto Valdez
Sarah Vargas

1924

Anita Arellano
Pablo Flores
Bolivar Martínez
Lawrence Redman
José B. Trujillo
Lafayette Varela
Cornelio Vigil

1929

Simmie Atencio (Santa Cruz)
Pauline Goddard (El Rito)
Richard Ortega (Chimayó)
Olive Parker (El Rito)
Raymond Romero (Vadito)
Cruz Trujillo (Chimayó)
José M. Valdez (Lyden)

1932

Lorencíta Chávez
J. Fernando Cruz
Casimira Gonzáles
E. Otila Gonzáles
Heranando J. Gonzáles
Calicia Griego
Faustina Gurulé
Fay Marie Hembree
Manuelita Herrera
Trinidad López
Pedro Maestas
Frederick Martínez
Guillermo Martínez
Nellie Miranda
J. Amado Trujillo
Samuel Trujillo

1933

Margarita Abeyta
Presciliano Alire
Branche Viola Bull
Nicholas Candelaria
Martinianeau Felix
Edward Earl Goodwin
Isaac Gurulé
Juan Francisco Lobato
Alberto López
Stella López

Pedro Tomás Lucero
Thomas Allen Martin
Elena Estella Martínez
José Elías Romero
Juan Pedro Romero
Lydia Valdez
Mati Anita Vigil
Harriet Eluisa Weaver
Hasell Ward Weaver

1934

María Florentine
    Archuleta
Gilberto Archuleta
Natividad Atencio
Margaret Allen
    DesGeorges
José Isaac Domínguez
Ernestine F. Durán
Juan Antonio García
Salomon García
Michael Garner
Herbert Doyle Johnson
José Abbot Jaramillo
David Jaramillo
George A. Lobato
Pedro López
Isidoro Lucero, Jr.
Juan Francisco
    Manzanares

Carlos Martínez, Jr.
Elisa Ortíz
Beatrice Mae
    McKinnrey
María Cordelia Ortíz
Rosa Cecilia Ortíz
María Dolores Montoya
Amadeo Romero
Agneda Sánchez
María Irene Sánchez
Juan Ray Sena
José Lucas Trujillo
Cruz U. Valdez

1938

Ernestine Cora Alarid
Eugene Chacón
Mike A. Chacón
Ramona Chávez
Cordilia Córdova
Mary E. Daggett
Dan G. García
William Fred Gilliam
Joe A. Gonzáles
Ida Herrera
Joseph A. Luchetti
Dilia Manzanares
Fermín Presiliano
    Manzanares
Magdalena
    Manzanares
Severo Martínez
Manuel Eustaquio
    Medina
Preddie Medina

María L. Montoya
Joe F. Ortíz
Úrsula Ortíz
Ernest Quintana
Grace Sánchez
Manuel D. Sánchez
Victor F. Sánchez
María Eloisa
    Santistevan
Albert Curtis Thatcher
Amelia Trujillo
Cleofas L. Trujillo
Waldo Velásquez
Alonzo Henry Vigil
Mary Laura Vigil
Paul R. Vigil

1939

Jewell Irene Allison
Eduvigen Archuleta
Margarito Alex
    Archuleta
Jimmie J. Billia
James T. Cage, Jr.
Eleno Candelaria
Julia Chacón
Magin Rosina Chávez
Celestine Jaramillo
Lucas Jaramillo
Sam Jaramillo
John A. Martin
Juan M. Martínez
Marie Celina Martínez
Malaquías Martínez
Onesimo G. Martínez

Patrocino Martínez
Salomon Mascareñas
Cardenio C. Montoya
Flora Montoya
Rosinda Cordilia
    Rivera
Marcelino M. Sánchez
John Scarborough
Edward Varoz, Jr.
Albert J. Villarreal
Eliseo G. Vigil
José Eduardo Vigil

Class of 1941

Adela Pacheco
Clorinda Manzanares
Antonia Herrera
Elaiza Gonzáles
Regina Manzanares
Mary Frances Sánchez
Dora Atencio
Emma Jo Ball
Lawrence Velásquez
Abedón Varoz
Benito Valdéz
Ross Roybal
Robert Herrera
Antonio Chávez
Reducindo Chávez
Tony Manzanares
Sarah Jácquez
Stella Norris
Helen Espinoza
Lucille Wasson
Alma Banowsky

Eloisa Casados
Ernestine Lucero
Liberato Quintana
Fred Sandoval
Fiore Luchetti
Tommy Foster
Jack Roberson
Berny Valdez
Billy Hartwell
Jane Goddard
Cristóbal Lavadie
Lawrence García

Class of 1942

Helen Crume
Daniel Martínez
Arturo Gallegos
Aniceto Varoz
Matías Chacón
Tony Rivera
J. L. López
Kathryn Stanturf
Ted Varoz
Mildred Córdova
Modesto Vigil
Gwen Barrett
Esther Baca
Joseph Martínez
Louise López
J. V. Suazo
Cleo Flóres
Leon O'Neal
Ralph Chávez
Faye Stewart
Juliette Mente

Salomon Tafoya
Tony Perea
Margaret Martínez
Joe Leyba
Connie Sena
Faye Wynn
Sabino García
Mack Scarborough

Class of 1943

Donald Evans
Della Mente
Leopoldo Trujillo
Cruzita Olguín
I. B. Pickett
Cleo Archuleta
Bernice Domínguez
Epimenio Baca
Wanda Harris
Fred Jácquez
Maria D. Gonzáles
Martín Jaramillo
Tina Córdova
Dan Lovato
Martin Chase
Ofelia Ortega
Alex Salazar
Alice Varoz
Louise Vigil
Polly C. García
Nick García
Margaret Luján
Rubén Miera
Gordon Darling
Billie B. Johnson

Pat Martin
Alfredo Aguirre
Manuel García
Trinidad Griego
Lizzie Le Doux
Mary Sánchez
Ubaldo Vigil
Ida Johnson
Ambrosio Martínez
Cecilia Sena

Class of 1944

Martha Archuleta
Mela Baca
Jeanne Belknap
José Fernández
Dulcinea Girón
Joe R. Gonzáles
Tony Griego
Antonio Herrera
Teofila Jácquez
Isabel Jaramillo
Carmen Lucero
Alfonso Luján
Johnny Manzanares
Ramona Martínez
Helen Jo Medina
Eva Dean Roberson
Neva Jean Roberson
Paul Romero
Leonor Torres
Isabel G. Trujillo
Joe Trujillo
Angela Velarde

Class of 1945

Filemon Lovato
Julia Jaramillo
Rubén Manzanares
Irma Sisneros
Rufina Gallegos
Carlos López
Priscilla Rael
Manuela Vigil
Olivia Luján
Cora Martínez
Consuelo Manzanares
Gloria Vouterin
Ralph García
Margaret Atencio
Carroll Walsh
Lawrence Martínez
Clorinda Suazo
Elías Quintana

Class of 1946

Louise Abeyta
Leona Adams
Loyola Aragón
Pearl Bacalski
Helen Mendoza
Albinita Maestas
Frances Sánchez
Aurora Cisneros
Lorencita Barela
Camilo E. Medina, Jr.
Gilbert Martínez
Antonia Vigil
Elsie Rael

Malaquías Rael
Loretta Martínez
Orlinda Trujillo
Theodore Kuntz
Thomas Lavadie
Louise Naranjo
Veroniz Lucero
Michael García
Candelaria Martínez
Rumaldo Miera
José M. Herrera
Rudolfo Jaramillo
Ernesto Martínez
William Scarborough
Bernie Jaramillo

Class of 1947

Leo Apodaca
Elfego Aranda
Lupe Chávez
Lena Cisneros
Albert Domínguez
Cora I. Eichtle
Lloyd Englebrecht
Leo Fernández
Frankie Gallegos
Mike Gallegos
Dolores Gómez
Reyes Gonzáles
David Grant
Ernest Gurulé
Fabiola Jaramillo
Gilbert Jaramillo
Ross López
Richard Malooly

Pauline Manzanares
Juanita Márquez
Andrés Martínez
Anita E. Martínez
Annie Martínez
Atanacio Martínez
Chris Martínez
Rosina Mendoza
Mary Jean Mondragón
Leo Montoya
Margaret Ortíz
Concy Romero
Sam Romero
Francis Roybal
Edward Salazar
Helen Sánchez
Isabel Sánchez
George Sandoval
Alice Trujillo
Marcia Trujillo
Ramona Trujillo
Eleanor Vigil

Class of 1948

Eva Aragón
John Aragón
Cliseria Archuleta
Amelia Baca
Geneva Baca
Edward Birmingham
Audoro Campos
Roy Carrejo
Carmen Chacón
Belen Espinoza
Porfirio Frésquez

Flora Gallegos
Rose Gallegos
Ramona Gonzáles
Hilda Gutiérrez
Cristóbal Jaramillo
Anna Mae King
Juanita Lucero
Gilbert Maestas
Rosalie Manzanares
Gonzalo Martínez
Olando Martínez
Mary Mascareñas
Jean McCoy
Lillian Mondragón
Beau Newbern
Anna Ocaña
Dolores Rodríguez
Generaro Roybal
Dorothea Russ
Hannah Suazo
Norberto Trujillo
Mary A. Valdez
Adelia Vigil
Pat Vigil

Class of 1949

Lucy Archuleta
Madge Baca
Nick G. Baca
Betty Jo Carnes
Elsie García
Filemon García
Lila García
Preciliano García
Tony García

Berniece Gonzáles
Billy Gonzáles
Irene Herrera
Delourdes Jácquez
Anastacio Lobato
Cassie Márquez
Eduardo Martínez
Isabella Martínez
Robert Mascareñas
Carl Naranjo
Joan Odom
Lourdes Pacheco
Fred Rael
Ermelina Romero
Tillie Sisneros
Leo R. Suazo
Mary Trujillo
Susie Trujillo
Lila Valdez
Theresa Vigil

Class of 1950

Rubén Archuleta
Leo Sánchez
Consuelo Trambley
Wanda Adams
Clotario Archuleta
Orlando Arellano
Ernie Dow
Laura Branch
Rosalie Chávez
Charlie García
Ralph Gallegos
Marcella Durán
Bernie Gallegos

Elias Hurtado
Eloise Gallegos
Albiar Jaramillo
Tony Lucero
Eva Gallegos
Frances García
Salomon Martínez
Sally García
Elizario Montoya
Ben Roybal
Stella O. Gallegos
Marcia Hurtado
David Thatcher
Soraida Lucero
Indalesio Torres
Luis J. Trujillo
Helen Madrid
Fabiola Manzanares
Ernie Vigil
Mary Gloria Márquez
Mary Martínez
Olivia Martínez
Virginia Mondragón
Frances Moya
Kathie Price
Florence Quintana
Lucy Roybal
Rosina Salazar
Celia Sisneros
Angie Varela
Gilbert Vigil
Isidore Vigil
Juan Vigil
Richard Rael
Ernestine Rael
Raymond Rodriguez

Class of 1951

Evangeline Martínez
Laurence Smith
Eremita Salazar
Tony Montoya
Beva Manzanares
Danny Chávez
Joe Fernández
Orilia Vigil
Donald Hatch
Evangeline
    Manzanares
Horacio Jaramillo
Marie Sánchez
Rose Lucero
Luis Baca
Consuelo Moya
Azucena Lobato
Steve Archuleta
Abel Gómez
Stella Manzanares
Joe Jaramillo
Corine Sánchez
Rose Rivera
Susan McCoskey
David Smith
Helen L. Valdez
Leonard Trujillo
Claudina Manzanares
Arcelia Vigil
Orlando Peña
Lisbeth Giddings

Class of 1952

Theresa Baca
Roman Chacón
Pete Chávez
Terry Crider
Irene Delgado
Fern Harris
Alfonso Jaramillo
Benito Juárez
Mary Margaret Lobato
Libradita Lucero
Fred Mares
Johnny Molina
Johnny Molina
Roman Mondragón
Celina Ortíz
Saby Rimbert
Ruby Rivera
Lucy Trujillo
Arturo "Casey"
    Martínez
Regino Salazar
Mary Valencia

Class of 1953

Charlie Aragón
Joella Archuleta
Lorraine Archuleta
Lawrence Barone
Katie Bateman
Flora Dominguez
Archie Dow
Carmen Durán
Amalia Espinoza

Elizabeth Lobato
Pete Lobato
Maxine Lucero
Rosina Lucero
Ruben Lucero
Josephine Maes
Marie Maes
Angelina Martinez
Beatrice Martínez
Florence Mondragón
Tony Montoya
Raul Martínez
Albert Romero
Eddie Sisneros
Adelia Trujillo
Sencionita Varoz
Ermelinda Trujillo

Class of 1954

Julia Archuleta
Salomon Archuleta
Mary Baros
Dorothy Bateman
David Borunda
Michael Branch
Jimmy Chávez
Lourdes Espinoza
Sammy Esquibel
Reyna   Gonzáles
Richard García
Elva Jaramillo
Mike Jaramillo
Mel Lobato
Delfinia Lucero
Delia López

Ernestine Lucero
Urcinia Lucero
Betty Maes
Toribio Manzanares
Joe Martínez
Rafaelita Martínez
Gloria Ortíz
Simmie Romero
Dennis Salazar
Tim Sánchez
Theresa Sandoval
Manuel Torres
Aurelia Trujillo
Prescilla Trujillo
Barbara Valdez
Joe Valdez
Helen N. Valdez
Mary Vigil
Oralia Vigil

Roman López
Felix López
Denny Lucero
Savino Lucero
Sylvia Lucero
Laura Lucero
Ted Martínez
Ida Peña
Rosemary Romero
Lee Sisneros
Leroy Martínez
Ernestine Trujillo
Olivia Trujillo
Mary Lou Trujillo
Patsy Trujillo
Peggy Trujillo
Viola Trujillo
Eli Valdez
Amarante Varoz

Josie Lucero
Isaura Maes
George Maestas
Dora Maestas
Orlando Manzanares
Estolano Márquez
Tito Martínez
Josie Ocaña
Norma Ordoñez
Florence Ruiz
Johnny Sánchez
Olivia Salazar
Katherine Tafoya
Sylvia Tafoya
Robert Torres
Abedon Trujillo
Eloy Trujillo
Reyna Velarde
Nancy Lee Vigil

Class of 1955

Alfonso Archuleta
Louise Archuleta
Mary Atencio
Viola Ávila
Esperanza Baca
Arnold Boggus
Emma Duran
Jo Ann Durán
Albert Esparcen
Manuel Ferran
Arlene Gonzáles
Lupe Juárez
Horacio Archuleta
Lorraine Gonzáles

Class of 1956

Leo Archuleta
Socorro Baca
Chris Delgado
Orlando Dow
Ray Esquibel
Vangie Frésquez
Gerald Garcia
Eliseo Griego
Lydia Jaramillo
Sabine Griego
Santiago Jaramillo
Gerald Lewis
Horace López
Agustina Lucero

Class of 1957

Polly Abeyta
Cecilia Archuleta
Florida Archuleta
Lydia Archuleta
Virginia Archuleta
David Baca
Erlinda Baca
Gloria Baca
Tom Bachicha
Janet Boggus
Dennis Branch
Sara Mary Chávez
Celedón Espinoza
Otilia Esquibel

Leo García
Olivia Gómez
Cecilia Gutierrez
Eligio Jaramillo
Lee Leyba
Josie Lucero
Gilbert Maestas
Sigfredo Maestas
Pete Manzanares
Richard Manzanares
Vivian Manzanares
Lugie R. Martínez
Susie Martínez
Phil Miera
Ida Montoya
Joe Ortega
Pete Romero
Arthur Sánchez
Louie Sánchez
Porfirio Sánchez
Dorothy Trujillo
Connie Valdez
Tito Valdez
Armida Velarde
Nancy Zamora

Class of 1958

Celerino Archuleta
Mel Archuleta
Robert Archuleta
Ramón Baca, Jr.
Servilia Baca
Rudy Cornay
Patricia Esquibel
Virginia García

Olivia Gonzáles
Nila Jaramillo
Evila Lobato
Viola López
Catherine Manzanares
Rosalie Montoya
Augustine H. Martínez
Richard Martínez
Ross Martínez
Helen Medina
Cora Ortega
Dulcie Peña
Chris Quintana
Mary Katherine
    Romero
Joe Stanley Sánchez
Henry Serrano
Rey Sisneros
David Trujillo
Drucella Trujillo
Lucas Trujillo
Lucille Trujillo
Robert Trujillo
Gilbert Varoz

Class of 1959

Criselda Archuleta
Rudy Archuleta
Arthur C. de Baca
Mary Branch
Gloria Bustos
Elizaida Campos
Adan García
Gilbert García
Lucille Gonzáles

Eloisa Jaramillo
Johnny Jaramillo
Rudy Jaramillo
Alex Loomis
Rubén Lovato
Mae Rose Maestas
Adolfo Manzanares
Carmen Manzanares
Eloisa Manzanares
Grace Márquez
Frido Martínez
Mary Martha Martínez
Ralph Martínez
Sammy Martínez
Leroy Mondragón
Carlos Ortega
Lía Ortega
Cecilia Romero
Gilbert Sisneros
Rudy Sisneros
Luis Torres
Cándido Trujillo
Mike Trujillo
Louis Velarde
Randy Velarde
Elvira Vigil
Frances Vigil

Class of 1960

Mary Frances Apodaca
Bertina Archuleta
Johnny Atencio
Leon Baca
Florinda Campos
Cleo G. Chávez

Mary Alice Cornay
Manuel Corrales
Phil Flóres
Pete García
Ninfa Griego
Erlinda Gonzáles
Ralph Herrera
Priscilla Jaramillo
Raymond Lobato
Fabiola Lucero
Odelia Lucero
Roberta Lucero
Dora C. Martínez
Judy Martínez
Gilbert Mascareñas
Criselda Ortíz
Robert Romero
John David Sánchez
Raymond Sánchez
Isaac Serrano
Leroy Silva
Herman Trujillo
Marie Trujillo
Rebecca Trujillo
Joseph Valdez
Esmael Valerio
Betty Varoz
Lorraine Vigil
Robert Vigil

Class of 1961

Liova Archuleta
Marie Archuleta
Sally Archuleta
Patricia Baca

Alfred Barboa
Larry Barela
Priscilla Carrillo
Freddie Chávez
Robert Córdova
Leo Estrada
Arthur Griego
Alice Gutiérrez
Helen Gutiérrez
Theresa Lobato
Susie López
Pablo Maestas
Patricia Nieto
Dillio Ocaña
Sulema Ortega
Julian Padilla
Robert Romero
Ernest Santistevan
Jack Sena
Barry Stewart
Joan Trujillo
Joe Trujillo
Gilbert Valdez
Gene Varoz
Sifredo Martínez
Ruben Varela

Class of 1962

Diana Archuleta
Bertha Baca
Milnor Branch
Beva García
Juliet García
Amabel Gonzáles
Cecilia Gonzáles

Joe Gilbert Gonzáles
Lawrence Gutiérrez
Janet Klimka
Stella Candelaria
Annabell López
Mary Manzanares
Catherine Ann (Cam)
    Martin
Cora Martínez
Fredy Martínez
Bertram Peña
Ernest Peña
Rosie Quintana
Virginia Rimbert
Johnny Romero
Robert Rosales
Raymond Valdez
Peter Valdez
Amelia M. Vigil
Louise Domínguez
Douglas Mahaney

Class of 1963

Betty Atencio
James Baca
Johnell Carson
Oralia Chávez
Archie Crump
Benny Córdova
Helen Ferran
Beverly Gallegos
María Dolores
    Gonzáles
Billy Jaramillo
Loretta Maes

Gloria Manzanares
Tony Márquez
Cecilia Martínez
Rosabel Martínez
Flora Moya
Allen Nickelson
Robert Rivera
Marian Sánchez
Marcia Valdez
Sue Ann Valencia
Cordy Varoz
Richard Velásquez

Class of 1964

Gladys Archuleta
Sam Archuleta
Silviano Archuleta
Henry Baca
Johnny Baca
Bob Couch
John Dantis
Nick Dantis
Roger Davis
John Esquivel
Sherry Fribley
Barbara Ann García
Jane Gómez
Teofilo Madrid
Tommy Martin
Sandra Gonzáles
Roger Valdez
David Padilla
Stella Holmes
Marianne Valdez
David Valdez

Mary Agnes Griego
Oliver Vigil, Jr.
Maxine Gallegos
Napoleon Quintana
Milfred Martínez
Mercy Sandoval
Joe Martínez
Simmie García
Arturo Sisneros
Gilbert López
George Ann Vigil
Mike Salazar
Esther Sánchez
William Gonzáles
Ruth Salazar
Nancy Martínez
Alonzo García
Mary Ortíz
Dolores Martínez
José Rosario López

Class of 1965

Pauline Alire
Corine Archuleta
Peter Archuleta
Jimmy Atencio
Joseph Baca
Lawrence Baca
Albert Carrillo
Joe Córdova
Sam García
Mary Jane López
Carlos Martínez
Clarence Jaramillo
Severo Padilla

Leo Griego
Palmeria Quintana
Bobby Joe Gonzáles
Joann Martínez
Toby Lucero
Helen Harman
Adelina García
Roger Martínez
Cordy Lucero
Alfonso Trujillo
Ben Trujillo
Bertha Angela Trujillo
Billy A. Trujillo
Danny Trujillo
Cindy Hernandez
Fabian Martínez
Bertha Lucero
Ricky Martínez
Johnny Griego
Sam Salazar
Tito Ortíz
Frances Romero
Larry Rogers
Rudy Martínez
Barbara Valdez
Marcella Valdez
Sandra Vigil
Ernest Yanez

Class of 1966

Andy Archuleta
Bertha Archuleta
Florencio Archuleta
Sonny Ford
Arnold Gallegos

Cecilia García
Dolores García
Gerry García
Alfred Gonzáles
Rudy Jaramillo
Alice Lovato
Juanito Lovato
Alfonso Lucero
Sonny Maes
Mary Márquez
Chris Martínez
Cruz Martínez
Dorothy Martínez
Marcella Martínez
Mary Toni Martínez
Tony Mauro
Juanita Ocaña
Michael Ortíz
Leroy Salazar
Edith Valdez
Leo Valdez
David Varoz
Lucy Varoz

Class of 1967

Herman Abeyta
Susie G. Alire
Hilbert Archuleta
Presciliano Archuleta
Toby Archuleta
Phillip Branch
Diane Brewster
Roberta Campos
Georgina S. Chávez
Leo G. Cisneros

Fred DeVargas
Mabel Díaz
Rosemary Díaz
Donna Ellen Gallegos
Eileen Dorothy
    Gallegos
Joe García
Lawrence J. García
Janet Goddard
Eddie Gutiérrez
Ricky Gutiérrez
Josie López
Ponciano Madrid
Joseph Emery Maes
Tito Maestas
Steve Mantel
Barnie Martínez
Lito Montoya
Michael J. Ortíz
Serafin Padilla
Arthur Rodarte
Anthony Sandoval
Richard Sisneros
Jo Ann Trujillo
Richard Trujillo
Robert Valdez
Kathleen Vigil
Bud Vizcaíno

Class of 1968

Prescilla Alire
Charlene Archuleta
Donald Archuleta
Ruben Archuleta
Pamela Atencio

Yolanda Atencio
Lorraine Blea
Anthony Chacón
Chris Chávez
Alex García
Robert Goddard
Dolores Gonzáles
Johnny Gonzáles
Stanley Griego
Christine Gutiérrez
Gloria Herrera
Guzman Jaramillo
Cornelio López
Elma López
David Lucero
Raymond Lucero
Ralph Maes
Veronica Maes
Pauline Martínez
Phyllis Martínez
Prescilla Moya
George Peña
Arthur Romero
Marquita Sena
Jerome Torres
Catherine Valdez
Michael Valdez
Ramona Valdez
Josephine Ybarra

Class of 1969

Victor Chávez
Pamela García
Lydia Gutiérrez
David Jaramillo

Corine Lucero
Irene López
Anthony Manzanares
Greg Martin
JoAnne Martínez
Theresa Martínez
Judy Morales
Richard Romero
Benjie Trujillo
Eva Trujillo
Melva J. Trujillo
Steven Valdez
Isabel Vigil
John Wilkins
Linda Wilkins

www.ingramcontent.com/pod-product-compliance
Lightning Source LLC
Chambersburg PA
CBHW022008080426

42733CB00007B/524